STOIC, CHRISTIAN AND
HUMANIST

STOIC, CHRISTIAN AND HUMANIST

by

GILBERT MURRAY

Essay Index Reprint Series

BOOKS FOR LIBRARIES PRESS
FREEPORT, NEW YORK

First Published 1940
Reprinted 1969

STANDARD BOOK NUMBER:
8369-1363-9

LIBRARY OF CONGRESS CATALOG CARD NUMBER:
75-99712

PRINTED IN THE UNITED STATES OF AMERICA

Preface

THE essays in this book are in part the results of special reading and study. I have worked a good deal at various times on problems of ancient religion and modern anthropology, and at one time when I was invited to give the Gifford Lectures on Natural Religion I thought of making a systematic attempt at a statement of my *Weltan-schauung*, comprising a profound belief in ethics and disbelief in all revelational religions. I append a note on a few of the specialist books that I have found helpful.

In another aspect, however, the essays are merely by-products of a long life in which I have had almost constantly in the back of my mind, as a half-conscious preoccupation, the aspirations, problems and moral compulsions which form part at least of the substance of religion.

I do not know if my experience is at all peculiar. But I believe my reaction toward the traditional religion of the society in which I was born falls into three periods. It began entirely as a moral rebellion in early childhood. Oddly enough, it was the miracle of the Gadarene swine that first shocked me. I cannot be sure of my age at the time, but it was before I left Australia and therefore before my eleventh birthday. It seemed to me so monstrously cruel to drive—or be indirectly responsible for driving—a lot of unoffending pigs over a precipice. It was just the sort of thing I could imagine being done by very wicked boys, the kind of boys that tortured animals and loved bullying. The germ of criticism once admitted, I began in my teens to be uneasy about other elements in the New Testament: the unreasonable cursing of the fig-tree, the doctrine of eternal damnation, and the whole conception of vicarious atonement. What could a schoolboy think of a master who, when offended, made no particular difference between the guilty and the innocent, but insisted on his right to flog somebody?

It seems to me, as I look back, that I was a very innocent and perhaps priggish boy, crudely humanitarian and idealist. The cruelty to animals in my school in the bush almost drove me mad. I had many fights about it. And there were other things I hated almost as much. When first, by mere accident, I came across the writings of Shelley I was almost dazzled by finding suddenly the expression of my own unspoken dream. This, I felt, was the right thing. This was what I wanted, what I craved for. It was the antidote to all the coarseness and brutality and contempt for weaker creatures which raged round about me.

I do not mean that I was on the whole unhappy at my Australian school. The spirits of the young are mercurial. I liked my masters, enjoyed most of my lessons, and loved cricket. But I began even then to feel that it was no good talking to the authorities, clerical and other, about the scruples or ideals that moved me most. Certainly I was always too shy to think of explaining myself.

The intellectual reasons for disbelief came to me much later. Here I was influenced not so much by the obviously unscientific character of the accounts of the creation and other stories in the Old Testament, as by the discovery that different nations had different religions, and by a subsequent comparative study of religion and anthropology. I found that every successive civilization has had its own explanation of the world. Each has claimed to be, alone and exclusively, the Way, the Truth and the Life. The explanations have varied as the civilizations varied, and passed away as the civilizations passed. It was, for instance, simply due to historical causes that Europe became Christian and Asia Minor Moslem, and that England, for instance, adopted its particular form of Christianity. Consequently it seemed improbable that the particular country and age in which I happened to be born had received an exclusive revelation of the truth.

Besides that, in my later school days and

early years as an undergraduate, I continued to feel that the rather conventional clergymen who formed the majority of my teachers were not very inspiring, not people to whom one could talk freely of serious things. The best and most interesting people I knew were Freethinkers. It was not till I came to know Charles Gore, afterwards Bishop of Oxford, that I discovered that extreme orthodoxy was compatible not merely with great charm and intellectual power but with a most sensitive humanity and generosity of outlook. This strong high-churchman was, I found, quite as good a man as the two or three radical Freethinkers whom I adored and towards whom I still feel a profound affection and gratitude. I ceased forthwith to be anti-clerical, though I did not seriously change my beliefs or disbeliefs.

The World War and events in post-war Europe have revealed a vast and awful gulf between the "ideologies" or, as I should prefer to say, the fundamental faiths of different kinds of men. The gulf stares us in the face; it is of enormous importance, but it is hard to define. It is certainly not a mere clash between Socialism and capitalism, between Conservatism and a desire for change, between democracy and some other political system. Nor yet is it between Christianity and scepticism. Lenin's Russia is anti-

God. Franco's Spain is devoutly Catholic. The German Government is partly Christian, partly Pagan; the Japanese Government Shinto-Buddhist: but much the same foul deeds have been done, and not only done but admired and glorified, by all of them. The revolt of the human conscience against such cruelties has been often no doubt Christian versus non-Christian, but much more consistently Liberal versus militarist. If many of us cannot help feeling in the world about us what Coleridge felt in his nightmare—

> "A lurid light, a trampling throng,
> Sense of intolerable wrong,
> And what I scorned, that only strong":

it is impossible to identify "that which we scorn" with any particular orthodoxy or unorthodoxy. One is often reminded of Mr. Gladstone's phrase, "the denial of God erected into a system of Government", and tempted to describe the conflict, in broader terms, as a clash between religion in some sense and an utter denial of the fundamental elements of religion. Yet even this conception is not quite satisfying, because if a certain lowering of standards and an acceptance of money values as more important than moral values may be due to lack of religion, the worst actual abominations of the time are due to various forms of fanaticism, a fanaticism sometimes religious, sometimes political, but strangely similar to that which raged in the Religious Wars. One can perhaps truly say that what is being endangered in Europe is what people call "the Christian spirit"; but that phrase will mean the Christian spirit as humanized and liberalized in the nineteenth century, a spirit totally different from that of the hell-ridden persecuting Christianities of various past ages. I would just as soon call it "a humane spirit" or "a Liberal spirit". We call it Christian because when our own conscience rejects some action we like to find some authority for our feeling. We say that Jesus or St. Francis would condemn it, just as a Chinese would appeal to Confucius or an ancient Roman to the philosophers:

"Chrysippus non dicet idem, nec mite Thaletis
Ingenium, dulcique senex vicinus Hymetto,
Qui partem acceptae dura inter vincla cicutae
Accusatori nollet dare."

No doubt the higher moral effort of man in every nation will, for the great majority, express itself in the traditional religious conventions of that nation. Moral idealism in England will be for the most part Protestant, in Austria Catholic, in Turkey Moslem, in China Confucian or Buddhist. But in the more civilized communities, as in ancient Greece, there has always been a minority who, through some speculative urge in their own minds or perhaps through the circumstances of their lives, have felt convinced that the traditional frame of dogmas current about them did not represent the exclusive truth, the necessary truth, or even any exact truth at all about the ultimate mysteries, and have tried to keep their sense of the duty of man towards his neighbour and his own highest powers clear of the confusing and sometimes perverting mythology on which it is traditionally said to be based. Its real basis is the rock of human experience.

What I have written in this little book may, I fear, alienate or at least pain some of the friends with whom I have worked most closely for certain great humane causes. They may ask why I should write such criticism at all. If I cannot positively help the faith of the average man, why can I not at least keep silent? My answer is that, if these subjects are of importance to mankind, as I believe them to be, it is our duty to seek the truth about them.

Contents

Bibliographical Note

On Pagan Religion and Philosophy

ROSTOVTZEFF, M. *The Social and Economic History of the Roman Empire.* Oxford University Press, 1926.

WENDLAND, PAUL. *Die Hellenistisch-Römische Kultur.* Third edition. Mohr, Tübingen, 1912.

CUMONT, FRANZ. *Les Religions Orientales dans le Paganisme Romain.* Fourth edition. Paris, 1929.

FRAZER, SIR J. G. *Adonis, Attis, Osiris.* Macmillan, 1906.

HARRISON, J. E. *Themis.* Second edition. Cambridge University Press, 1927.

MURRAY, GILBERT. *Five Stages of Greek Religion.* Oxford University Press, 1925.

CORNFORD, F. M., on "Mystery Religions and Pre-Socratic Philosophy" in the *Cambridge Ancient History*, vol. iv, and on "The Athenian Philosophical Schools", ib. vol. vi.

CORNFORD, F. M. *Greek Religious Thought* (selections translated). Dent, 1923.

BEVAN, EDWYN. *Later Greek Religion* (selections translated). Dent, 1927.

ROSS, W. D. *Aristotle* (selections translated). Oxford University Press, 1927.

NOCK, A. D., on "Early Gentile Christianity" in Rawlinson's *Essays on the Trinity and the Incarnation.* Longmans, 1928.

NOCK, A. D. *Conversion.* Oxford, 1934.

FABRE, P. *Le Monde Greco-romain au temps de Notre Seigneur.* Paris, 1935.

GUTHRIE. *Orpheus and Greek Religion.* Cambridge, 1935. With full bibliography.

Celsi 'Αληθὴς Λόγος, by Glöckner, in Lietzmann's *Kleine Texte*, Bonn, 1924. This is an attempt to reconstruct

the philosopher Celsus's criticism of Christianity out
of the passages quoted from him in Origen's volu-
minous book *Against Celsus*.

BURKITT, F. C. *Jewish and Christian Apocalypses*, the Schweich
Lectures. Oxford University Press, 1914.

REITZENSTEIN, R. *Die Hellenistischen Mysterienreligionen*. Third
edition. Teubner, 1927.

KLOSTERMANN, ERICH. *Apocrypha I, Reste des Petrusevan-
geliums der Petrusapokalypse und des Kerugma Petri*. Bonn,
1908.

WEBSTER, HUTTON. *Primitive Secret Societies*. New York,
1908.

SCHURTZ, HEINRICH. *Altersklassen und Männerbünde*. Berlin,
1902.

DIETERICH, ALBERT. *Nekyia*. Teubner, 1898.

On Stoicism

(1) *Original Stoic Literature*

EPICTETUS. *Discourses*, etc., translated by P. E. Matheson.
Oxford, 1915.

MARCUS AURELIUS. *To Himself*, translated by J. Jackson.
Oxford, 1906.

Stoicorum Veterum Fragmenta, collected by Von Arnim,
Leipsig, 1903–1905.

(2) *Modern Literature*

ARNOLD, E. V. *Roman Stoicism*. Cambridge, 1911 (with large
bibliography).

BEVAN, EDWYN. *Stoics and Sceptics*. Oxford, 1913.

DUDLEY, D. R. *A History of Cynicism*. Methuen, 1937.

I

Pagan Religion and Philosophy at the Time of Christ

I

PAGAN RELIGION AND PHILOSOPhY
AT THE TIME OF CHRIST

I. RELIGION AND PHILOSOPHY

The life of man can be divided, like the old maps of the world, into the charted and uncharted. The charted is finite and the other infinite; yet for a well-situated member of a successful and peaceful civilization the part of life which is fairly subject to reason and control outweighs enormously the parts about which he cannot calculate. He can anticipate the results of most of his actions, can work at his profession, till his fields and and plant fruit trees, nay, even educate his children, with some reasonable expectation of success. He is guided by experience and reason: he values competent work and exact thought. He realizes his dependence on society, and accepts his duties towards it: he obeys the laws and expects to be protected by them. And such a man, when trying to form a conception of the universe or of life as a whole, will tend to do so in the same sober spirit, and regard the vague terrors and longings that sometimes obsess him as likely to be sources of error. Such a society, at its best, will produce science and philosophy.

It is different with a man who, through his own character or through circumstances, finds life beyond him. If the society in which he lives is torn by war and anarchy, or if he himself is very poor and ignorant, he can neither control his fortune nor understand why things happen to him. He is now taxed, now beaten, now enriched, now stricken with famine or pestilence, and such results do not seem to depend much upon ascertainable causes. His confidence in the charted regions grows less and he throws himself on the unknown. He feels from the beginning that he is in the power of incalculable beings or forces, and makes passionate, though uncertain, efforts at placating them. These efforts will be guided little by observation of the external world, and much by the man's own instincts and subconscious desires. They may lead to good conduct or bad, to high forms of religion or to degraded superstition. The frightened man may determine to give alms to the poor, or to pay his debts, or even to live in mystic contemplation. He may be content to persecute heretics or to perform filthy and cruel rites.

There is nobody, of course, whose mind is devoted entirely to the charted region, nor yet to the uncharted. To the most rational and sober of men there must come from time to time a consciousness of the presence all round him of undiscovered and perhaps undiscoverable forces, a vast night surrounding the small illuminated patch in which he moves; while to the most blindly superstitious a very large part of his daily life must be conducted on principles of observation and reason. The deadest rationalist has some consciousness of mystery, the most helpless mystic some gleams of common sense. Still, on the whole, as society advances in security and human beings in intellectual culture, there is an increase in the range of knowledge and reason and the proportion which they occupy in life. As the social order decays and the level of culture falls, the irrational element in life grows and the little island of light amid the darkness grows smaller still.

When we speak of "ancient philosophy" as contrasted with "the Christian religion" we must realize that religion is something common to the highest and lowest of human societies, while philosophy has always been the attainment of a small class in a high state of culture. Philosophy implies a view of the world which uses the knowledge and thinking power of man to their utmost limit, though every good philosophy recognizes the limits of human intelligence and leaves room for the unknown beyond the border. When civilization decays philosophy must needs decay with it: a disintegrating society may produce an age of faith or one of brutal materialism, but it cannot well produce philosophy.

Among the various causes or symptoms of the decay of ancient civilization Professor Rostovtzeff has rightly emphasized the disappearance, through economic and political causes, of the cultured class. The governing class of the Roman Empire, originally drawn from senatorial families in Rome and Italy but afterwards from distant provinces as well, had not only a high tradition of public service, but also very considerable literary culture, while it commanded the services of highly skilled officials and technical assistants in every department of government. A dialogue of Plutarch, written in the early part of the second century A.D., describes the meeting at Delphi of cultured Roman citizens from the most diverse parts of the world, a Greek country gentleman, an administrator, a poet, a grammarian, a professor from Britain, much as, at the present day, one might find together in Cairo an English M.P., an American professor, a Scotch engineer, an Indian civilian, and a professional archaeologist—all of them, whatever their diversities of training or interest, united in the service of modern civilization. The Imperial cultured class may have been limited, but it had wide experience; it knew its business and, at this time, it felt perfectly secure. It took little interest in the beliefs of the vast unlettered proletariate beneath it. Plutarch, with all his variety of interests, never notices Christianity. Three centuries later Christianity was dominant, and the cultured class was in the last stage of dissolution. Synesius, the Platonist bishop of the Libyan tetrapolis, complains that he can find in his diocese almost no person who knows Greek or philosophy, no body of men who can be trusted to collect money for public purposes, no one who knows how to make good roads or weapons of war, or how to collect or command a competent military force to protect the settlement against the negroes of the interior. The careful agriculture on which the prosperity of the place depended was now above people's heads. The bishop's friend, Hypatia the Neoplatonist, was brutally murdered by the Alexandrian mob. The mob was now Christian, and less under control; but it had behaved in much the same way when it was pagan, and was just as far removed from "ancient philosophy".

We must remember, therefore, in making any comparison between Christianity and ancient philosophy, that Christianity belongs to a time when ancient culture was on the down grade and to a class which had always been shut out from it. The greater part of ancient philosophy originated in the fourth century B.C., before the free and highly cultivated city-states had been superseded by the large military empires, and their more or less manageable problems swamped in those of a limitless and undisciplined world. Philosophy weathered the storms of the Roman conquest and the civil wars, and became permanently the possession and guide of educated men without distinction of race or nation, but it hardly touched the uneducated. Thus, with some exceptions to be noticed hereafter, classical philosophy represents the view of society and of duty which is natural to men of position, with a sense of responsibility. Christianity, and the various passionate religions which competed with it in the great industrial towns, represented the aspirations of the poor and outcast.

These considerations explain the mutual indifference to one another of Christianity and ancient philosophy. The professor or administrator did not inquire what his foreign slaves talked about in the kitchen, nor did the slaves try to understand the books and papers which they were told not to disturb in the study. But sometimes, instead of this indifference, there was, in many places if not throughout the empire, a passionate hostility. Liberal pagans, who would not have thought of persecuting ordinary free speech, drew the line at Christians and sometimes at Jews. Christians who preached, and no doubt in some respects practised, a religion of meekness exhausted their vocabulary of curses against Rome. This needs some explanation.

The restoration by Augustus of peace and order after the civil wars was felt, not merely by flatterers or adherents, but by the whole law-abiding population of the Roman world, as something like a miracle of beneficence. It was impossible to prevent the Eastern Provinces, accustomed to such ideas, from worshipping Augustus as a god; and even Italy and the West gradually lost their repugnance to that exotic conception. The peace had really brought something like a heaven upon earth. And though Augustus might die and Tiberius stubbornly refuse to be worshipped, there was something divine which remained. It was Rome herself, "Rome the Goddess", "Rome the Benefactress". Together with the Emperors as her representatives, it was the spirit which made Caesar and Rome invincible, the *Genius*, the *Fortuna*. Rome meant peace, order, good government, and the welfare of man. Her old brutality had been greatly humanized by Greek philosophy. Rome was *caput orbis*, the "head" of which the whole world was the "body". She drew little or no distinction of race or nationality among her subjects or citizens, and the well-to-do classes throughout the world were ready, as a rule, to give her more worship than she claimed. For all she demanded was, on certain specified occasions, a prayer for the Fortune of Rome and Caesar, and a gift of incense at their altars. The act required meant little more than singing "God save the King", but it happened to be the very thing that most Christians and Jews could not give. For one thing, they could represent it to themselves as the worship of a false God. That scruple might perhaps have been met: but, more than that, it was the worship of something which they hated. For Rome had always had three types of enemy, the conquered nations, the predatory tribes and classes, and the oppressed proletariate within her own borders.

The Roman governing class, tamed and educated by Greece, had saved the ancient world, and their overthrow ruined it. Yet it must be remembered that, in spite of the humanity of their best men, their régime and the world order that it maintained involved not only slavery on a vast scale, but a system of much hardship to its poorer subjects and atrocious severity to those who rebelled. Where the interest of Rome or, as they called it, the peace of the world was endangered the Roman governing class stuck at nothing. It was always remembered how the mortally dangerous slave-revolt led by Spartacus was ended by the exhibition along the whole stretch of the Appian Way of six thousand crucified slaves. The free workman and peasant were also exposed to many of the abuses of capitalism and usury in their earliest and crudest forms. The sayings against the rich which abound in the Gospels, and the imprecations against the Roman Empire which fill the *Book of Revelation*, are echoes of many centuries of misery endured and resented by the proletariate of Italy and a large part of the whole populations of the conquered provinces. As Professor Arnold Toynbee has pointed out, when Jesus in the Gospel declares that "The foxes have holes and the birds of the air have nests, but the son of man hath not where to lay his head", he is only repeating the old aching cry of the dispossessed peasant in the very words uttered long before by Tiberius Gracchus (Plut., *Tib. Grac.* IX).

"Blessed are the poor, blessed are they that mourn, blessed are the meek, blessed they that hunger and thirst. . . . It is easier for a camel to go through the eye of a needle than for a rich man to enter into the kingdom of God." Blessings of the same purport, and perhaps of equally mysterious beauty, had doubtless been spoken in many different ages by many thousands of men whose mission was to comfort the poor, both pagan and Christian.

And it was not blessings alone that thus arose from the *ergastula* and the wasted farms. "Fallen, fallen is Babylon the Great, the harlot that sitteth upon seven hills, and is drunken with the blood of the saints . . . with her merchandise of gold and silver and precious stones and chariots and slaves and the souls of men. . . . In one day shall her plagues come, death and mourning and famine; and she shall utterly be burned with fire. She shall be trodden in the wine-press of the wrath of God and blood shall come out of the wine-press even unto the bridles of the horses, as far as a thousand and six hundred furlongs"—nearly as far, perhaps, as stretched the crosses of those slaves on the Appian Way. To any contented and loyal Roman citizen such imprecations must have seemed to be the ravings of a veritable "odium generis humani".

Almost as significant as the things said are those left unspoken. There are no blessings on the strong and unselfish administrator, on the governor who braves unpopularity and prevents corruption, on the judge who does strict justice without fear or reproach. These suffering people do not understand justice. They can only say, "Blessed are the merciful!" They would have little use for that inflexible "severity" which the kindly Cicero so specially admires in a judge.

How could the poor fishermen of the Galilean Lake or their followers in the slums of Antioch, who thought of tax-gatherers merely as wicked people and had never held or expected to hold any post of public responsibility, have understood the Roman ideal of public duty? The Roman moralists were enthusiastic about their general, Regulus. He had been taken prisoner by the Carthaginians together with other soldiers of noble family. The Carthaginians hoped to exact a highly profitable peace by means of these prisoners, and Regulus was sent back to Rome to negotiate, promising to return if the negotiation failed. He considered that the lives of the prisoners were not worth such a concession. He went to Rome, stated the Carthaginian terms, and argued that it was more in the interest of Rome to let the prisoners die. He convinced the Senate and returned voluntarily to Carthage where he was duly tortured to death. His "virtue", resolute self-sacrifice for a public object, would have seemed to the Galileans unintelligible and perhaps, since it involved the death of many people whom he might have saved, wicked. It is very interesting to compare Cicero's book, De Officiis (On Duty), with the precepts of the Gospel. Infinitely less sublime and moving, it also differs from the Gospels in being concerned with a whole range of duties, administrative, judicial and military, which are outside the experience or imagination of the Asiatic villager or artisan. Cicero, for example, accepts as an axiom that Virtuous Conduct hinges on four cardinal virtues: Wisdom, or "the pursuit and perception of truth"; Justice, i.e. "the preservation of human society by giving to every man his due and by observing the faith of contracts"; Fortitude, i.e. "the greatness and firmness of an elevated and unsubdued mind"; and lastly, "Moderation or Temperance in all our words and actions". One sees in every phrase the man of culture, the man with a stake in the country, the soldier, statesman and governor. Such men were not to be found in the class from which the Christian movement arose.

2. CULTURE AND IGNORANCE

Apart from this social difference between the early Christian literature and that of contemporary pagan philosophy, there is another marked difference between the habits of mind of the ignorant and of the cultured. When St. Paul was preaching in Athens his audience listened with interest until he spoke of the "resurrection of the dead", or more literally "the uprising of the corpses". Then they laughed. They were familiar with the doctrine of the immortality of the soul, but when this eloquent Asiatic tent-maker began to explain that the dead bodies would get up and walk, they could not take him seriously. And we can see that Paul himself felt troubled over the form of his doctrine, and had to explain it rather elaborately. It seems as if the physical Resurrection of the Body was the only form in which the doctrine of immortality could be grasped by the very ignorant populations of the villages and big manufacturing towns of Asia Minor. One may think of a cultivated theologian at the present day listening to a Salvation Army preacher or still more to a negro revivalist. The doctrine preached may be essentially what he believes himself, but the expression of it is suited to a cruder intelligence.

Ignorance, of course, was no more confined to the Christians than hatred of Rome was. The same lack of intellectual training can be seen in some pagan writings of late antiquity. Abstract terms, for example, become persons or concrete objects. It is said that, during the World War, a body of Russian peasants being told that the war was being continued for the sake of "annexation", and that "annexation" must be given up, took "Annexation" (Annexia) to be a princess of the Imperial house and set off to hang her. The negroes in certain of the Southern States when told, after the civil war, that they were at last to receive the suffrage, came to fetch it with wheelbarrows. In the same way in some late pagan documents "the providence (Pronoia) of God" becomes a separate power; "the wisdom of God" (Sophia), becomes "the divine Sophia" or "Sophia, the daughter of God", and even in one case gets identified with Helen of Troy. The doctrinal history of the conception "Logos", the "word" or "speech" of God, shows similar developments. The results of intense abstract thought can only be understood by following, in some degree, the same process: when handed over mechanically to a generation entirely unaccustomed to abstract thought they change their meaning. Here again the contrast is not so much between pagan and Christian, but between the society of Aristotle or of Cicero and that of the Gnostics or the slave congregations.

Of course the advantage is never altogether on one side. It is hardly necessary to remind ourselves that the Galilean fishermen, by the very simplicity of their lives, by the fact that they knew nothing of complicated social responsibilities or problems, retained a power of direct vision which is not only far more moving but may actually be more profound than the good judgement of those with more knowledge of life. The Sermon on the Mount, though not so useful as a handbook to a Proconsul, may clearly cut far deeper toward the roots of things than Cicero's *De Officiis*. Furthermore, the age of general decadence and shaken nerves which began just before the rise of Christianity and returned in the third century A.D., was remarkable for some extraordinary qualities. Conduct, as far as one can judge so difficult a matter, was not better than in fourth-century Athens or first-century Rome. It was probably worse. There was more brutality, weakness, cowardice and disorder. Yet there was at the same time a widespread thirst for some sort of spiritual salvation; a sense of the evil of the world and a desire, at any sacrifice, to rise above it and be saved. There was also, both in Christian and pagan, a conviction of the need of some gigantic effort to overcome the sins of the flesh. Ancient philosophy was always ascetic. But in this period there was a passionate asceticism which often took strange and unwholesome forms, and which it is the fashion nowadays to treat with ridicule; yet it was perhaps something like an instinctive biological necessity, if the European world was not to sink into a condition of helpless sensuality like that of some oriental and savage societies. If we judge the world of the Gnostics and early Christians by standards of good citizenship and intelligence, it is far below the Rome of the

Antonines or the Athens of Plato; if we bring them all before a Last Judgement to which this whole world is as dross and passionate aspiration counts for more than steady good character, the decision will be more doubtful.

3. PREVIOUS PHILOSOPHY : PLATO AND ARISTOTLE

The early philosophers of the sixth and fifth centuries B.C. were more like men of science with a strong taste for generalization. Their problems were concerned with the physical world: they made researches in geometry, geography, medicine, astronomy, natural history, and were apt to sum up their conclusions in sweeping apophthegms. "Moisture is the origin of all things."—(Thales.) "All things were together till Mind came and arranged them."—(Anaxagoras.) "All things move, nothing stays; all things flow." —(Heraclitus.) "All things perish into that from which they sprang. They pay retribution for their injustice one to another according to the ordinance of Time."—(Anaximander.) Socrates, the father of the Attic school of philosophy, turning away from natural science with its crude generalizations, concentrated his attention on man, and particularly on the analysis of ordinary speech and current ideas. People talked of "justice" and "courage"; of things being "beautiful" or "ugly"; but no one could tell him what these words meant. Socrates still remains a problematical figure. A humorist and a saint, a mocker and a martyr, he made different impressions on different people of his acquaintance, but evidently had extraordinary powers as a teacher. Certain doctrines, mostly paradoxical, can with some probability be attributed to him—e.g. that virtue is knowledge, but cannot be taught, and that no one does wrong willingly—but in the main he set himself not to inculcate his own doctrines but to elicit from his pupils the full consciousness of what they themselves really believed or knew. This explains how, in the next generation, many divergent schools of philosophic thought professed themselves followers of Socrates.

The most famous of his disciples, Plato, preserved to an extraordinary degree his master's aversion to dogmatism. A dialogue of Plato's hardly ever leads to a positive conclusion. It is always a discussion, not a pronouncement. It may reject many dogmas as demonstrably false; but it never claims to have reached the whole truth. It probes deeper than before, climbs higher, uses every means—similes, parables, jests and all the resources of a prose style which has never perhaps been equalled since for variety and eloquence—to suggest the sort of thing that the truth is likely to be, or the way in which we can get nearest to it, but it ends almost always on a note of question or wonder. The particular doctrine, however, which is especially associated with Plato, and has divided the world ever since, is a purely intellectual one.

The plain man feels quite certain of two classes of facts. He is sure that what philosophers call "the external world" exists; that is, if he is sitting on a chair before a table, and looking out of the window at a river, he is confident that these things exist. If he can see, feel, lift, the chair and table; if he can go outside and see the river from a different point of view and put his hand into it, he has tested his belief and is more certain than before. Then again he is perfectly certain that twice two is four, and (if he has learnt a little mathematics) that the three internal angles of any triangle are equal to two right angles. But here comes a difficulty. The two systems of certainties do not confirm one another: rather the reverse. The rule "twice two equals four" is seldom or never true of the external world. No actual set of four apples is exactly double a particular set of two apples: not only have all the apples different individual qualities, but, if you have very exact weighing machines, you will find that even in weight the real four is seldom or never double the real two. Also, such triangles as you meet in the real world never satisfy the rules of mathematics. Their sides are never straight, for example. They are only imitation triangles, useful as signs or symbols of the triangles that you really mean.

Then again, suppose you do find some statement which you can make with truth about an object in the external world—"this river is about six feet deep", "this coat is blue", "this is the man I met last year", when you come to observe the objects again you may find it no longer true: the river has dried up to five feet, the coat has lost colour in the sun, the man has certainly become different. The world is all flowing and changing: you can never be sure of it; whereas the mathematical or arithmetical rule stays unchanged. Twice two is still four, and the three internal angles are still equal to two right angles, though a deluge may in the meantime have swept over the world.

Two views of this difficulty are possible. One man may say: "The real things are these chairs and tables; the mathematical rules are merely hypothetical or abstract statements about them": i.e. statements which would be true if the objects were different, or which are true if we disregard certain factors in the problem. Thus "twice two equals four" is only true of the apples if we disregard the accidental differences between the apples, or would be true if the apples were all exactly alike. The mathematical rule is a convenient generalization, no more. This man would call himself a realist.

The Platonist, on the contrary, starts at the other end: for him the rule "twice two equals four", or the rule about the internal angles, is exactly true and always true. It is the real truth, and the fluctuating, imperfect objects which we meet in the external world are only images or imitations of reality—like reflections in a bad mirror, distorted to start with and transitory as well. The only way to reach truth is to concentrate on the ideal world. Thus, in mathematics you can never get on by merely counting or weighing the existing triangles and tables and chairs: you start with your principles of arithmetic and then by reason deduce the whole world of number. And it must follow that the same method will lead to truth in all other regions too.

If you want to know what Justice is, you will not get very far by observing the behaviour of a number of honest men. Among other difficulties, no actual honest man is perfectly honest: he is only an imitation in flesh of true Justice as the wooden triangle is an imitation in wood of the ideal triangle. You must first get a clear conception of Justice—as clear as your conception of "two" or of "triangle"; then you will be able to deduce with mathematical exactitude the true properties of Justice. Truth is to be found, not in this fluctuating world of sense perception, but in the world which is reached by thought, i.e. by a clear and strictly rational introspection. For if the question is raised how we know that twice two is four, or that things which are equal to the same thing are equal to one another, it seems to be by some sort of intuition or introspection, or, as Plato half metaphorically puts it, by "recollection" (*Anamnêsis*) from a previous life. As we look into our own minds and discover that "twice two is four", so we can discover with equal certainty that Justice is beautiful or that a son should honour his father.

The obvious criticism here is that Plato is transferring the methods suitable to a system of exact knowledge, like arithmetic, to a chaotic world of words half understood and ideas incapable of definition. We do know what we mean by "two", but we do not know what we mean by "justice" or "beautiful". Plato himself criticizes his own suggestion more than once, and is never carried away into dogmatism. But this way of thinking formed a dangerous heritage for Greek and early Christian thought. The philosophers tended to conceive all knowledge as analogous to mathematical knowledge, either entirely right or entirely wrong. They failed to recognize or admit that most of what we call knowledge is only an approximation to the truth. A realization of this fact, which to us seems obvious, might have saved the world many desperate heresies and persecutions.

It is sometimes said that everyone is born either a Platonist or an Aristotelian, but the opposition between the two philosophers is not nearly so sharp as this would suggest. Though Aristotle rejected the doctrine of Ideas and was himself more concerned with biology and various forms of the "humane" sciences than with pure mathematics, yet he started as a Platonist, and retained always a profound admiration for his master. One quality that strikes one in reading Aristotle is the desire of the great researcher and collector to have a philosophic framework into which all real facts will fit. He will not be inhospitable to the discoveries of physical science, as many idealist philosophers were; neither will he rest content with any contradiction of common sense; nor yet will he shut the door against any genuine spiritual experience. A system so all-embracing roused little of the fighting spirit which seems necessary to enthusiasm among the later pagan philosophers. Aristotle was respected but not adored. Consequently he was not hated. And he had his reward in having his system taken over by various Christian theologians, especially by Thomas Aquinas, as the almost complete basis of the philosophy of the new religion.

Aristotle denied the existence of Plato's world of Ideas—Justice and the number Two did not exist separately in "some heavenly place", but were in the objects of the sensible world. One discovered them by a process of "Induction" (*Epagôgê*). By experience of a number of particular cases, the mind grasps a universal truth about them, which then and afterwards is seen to be self-evident. It sees the "Idea" or the "Form" by means of a review of individuals, but the "Idea" or "Form" is not something separate. The object of science thus becomes classification and the discovery of the attributes of objects. A new animal, for example, has to be assigned to the right genus, and the right species, and then distinguished from others by the attributes that are essential to it. Through this system of thorough-going classification he seems to have arrived at his discovery of the syllogism, and thus laid the foundation of Logic. The syllogism is a form of reasoning consisting of two premisses and a conclusion, in which one term which is common to both premisses disappears. From the relation of *A* to *B*, and from *B* to *C*, you conclude the relation of *A* to *C*. This discovery has been extraordinarily fruitful, though perhaps Aristotle was too apt to regard it as the sole type of deductive reasoning. Again, in all existence he distinguished between "form" and "matter": a statue consists of so much wood or stone—matter—on which a particular form is impressed, a sword of so much iron worked into a particular form. Connected with this division was another, which not only answered certain ancient philosophic puzzles, but gave a characteristic quality to his whole system. Suppose you say, "That man sitting in the chair is Phidippides, the swift runner", how can you be speaking the truth? How can a man sitting down be a runner? Aristotle's answer is that the man is "in act" (*energeia*) sitting, but "in power" (*dunamis*) or "potentially" a runner, and the idea thus suggested became fruitful in many ways. A man or city or any object not only is what it actually is at the moment; it is also, "in power", all that it may become. That mass of stone in the quarry is potentially a temple; this child is potentially a sage or a patriot. Influenced by his studies in biology Aristotle is full of the idea of a perfect or characteristic form to which all life tends, each species working towards its own perfection. In theology, both pagan and Christian, this idea led to a conception of the universe as fulfilling the purpose of God, or, rather differently, striving towards God as "the desire of the World". In modern science it plays an important part in the theory of evolution.

This meagre sketch is intended merely to show the kind of problem with which ancient Greek philosophy was occupied, in the domain of logic and metaphysic. Natural science we have entirely omitted, but of ethics or moral theory we must treat more fully.

4. ETHICS IN PLATO

It may be that ethics form a derivative and secondary kind of philosophy, dependent at every turn on Logic and Metaphysic, since a man cannot know what is good without knowing what is true. Nevertheless the information that interests a historian most about any religion or philosophy is both how its professors behaved and how they thought they ought to behave. Now Greek ethics in the classical period stand apart from those of most ancient societies. Like those of Confucius, they are singularly untheological. The Hebrew in all his conduct considered whether he was obeying or disobeying the rules given to Moses by Jehovah, and knew that if he disobeyed them Jehovah would be "angry" and punish him. The rules might or might not be consistent with the welfare of humanity; that question should not be raised, and in any case the welfare of the Gentiles did not much matter.

The Greek philosophers, with few exceptions, considered conduct with an eye on the welfare of the community, and the way in which the citizen could best serve his State. True, if he committed some offence, such as betraying a trust, the indignation felt against it might depend on purely "moral" considerations—e.g. the amount of treachery, impiety, cruelty, etc., involved—and not on the mere amount of harm done to the city; but the ultimate problem of human conduct was the problem of producing welfare or good life for the community.

Even in Plato, where idealism reigns and the spring of all good conduct seems to be Erôs, or passionate Love, for the Idea of the Good—that one ultimate aim of all right desire—morality is always an affair of the citizen, not of the isolated man. It is in practice a relation of man to his fellows, though no doubt it may ultimately rest on a relation of the soul to God. It still surprises a modern reader when the great problem of the *Republic*—what Righteousness is—is answered by the elaborate and to our minds obscure process of constructing an imaginary Republic. The answer also is a paradox. Plato sees in the man and the State alike three elements: one that craves, one that fights, and one that thinks, and finds righteousness in a harmony between them. There is the element of natural desire—for food, drink, sleep, bodily pleasure and all that is bought with money; the "spirited element", which fights against that which seems evil or hostile to the man or the community; and the element of thought, which judges, reflects and knows. When all these three serve the common good in harmony the result is Righteousness both in man and city. We can make no attempt here to analyse the extremely subtle and not always consistent theory of morals which we find in Plato. Of all great philosophers he is the least dogmatic and the most suggestive. He also combines in a remarkable way the attitude of the statesman, adapting means to ends, and the saint, doing right in scorn of consequences. His two longest works, the *Republic* and the *Laws*, are both attempts at constructing an ideal constitution, and in real life he faced much hardship, danger and ridicule in trying to put his political projects into practice. Yet at the same time no one insists more eloquently on the principles that it is better to suffer wrong than to do wrong, better to be punished than not to be punished, and that it is better to be righteous than to seem righteous, even if the former leads to death on the cross, and the latter to every kind of human reward. In contrast to the common conceptions of the ancient Hebrews or of the modern vulgar, the Greek thinkers are never content to say, "Be righteous because you will be punished if you are not". They almost always keep a firm hold on two principles: one, that good conduct is conduct that is good for the community as a whole; the other, that if righteousness or wisdom is good, then it is good in itself, and not because it leads to rewards in other coin.

5. ETHICS IN ARISTOTLE

But the most characteristic philosopher of the Hellenic period is Aristotle. He is Greek in his *sophrosynê* or moderation; in his complete remoteness from primitive superstition; in his combination of intense intellectuality with human sympathy and interest in practical life; and in his essentially civic point of view.

His theology and metaphysic were largely taken over by Thomas Aquinas and used as the basis of mediaeval and modern Christianity. His political philosophy is still a mine of thought and information. His researches in the physical sciences have of course been superseded in different degrees. It is in his ethics or theory of conduct that we find the characteristics of Greek thought at their clearest.

In the first place, conduct is an art, the art of living, and like all the arts it has an aim. In each department of conduct it aims at "virtue" or "goodness" (ἀρέτη), and this is always, as in the other arts, an exact point or degree, a mean between too much and too little. As a musician can go wrong by striking a note too high or too low, too loud or too soft, so a man may be too daring or not daring enough, not generous enough or too generous. This combination of common sense and exact thinking is highly characteristic. As to the aim of this art as a whole, as the aim of medicine is health, or of strategy victory, so the aim of ethics is the good life. The art of private ethics aims at the good life for the individual, but is subordinate to public ethics, or politics, which has for its aim the good life of the community. Aristotle decides after some discussion that this "good" must be something aimed at in all kinds of action, it must be desirable for itself and not merely as a means to something else, it must be self-sufficing. It must be "an unhindered activity of the soul", and a fulfilment of the true function of man as man, as good harping, for instance, is the function of a harp player. It must obviously be an activity "in accordance with virtue" (i.e. as we should say, "on the right lines"): and, characteristically, Aristotle adds that it must be "in a complete life", for it cannot operate when a man is miserably poor or deprived of freedom. This unhindered activity of the soul he identifies with *Eudaimonia*—a word which is usually translated "happiness". It is worth remembering, however, that etymologically the English word "happy" means "lucky", the Greek *eudaimon* means "with a good Spirit or Daemon".

We may observe that such happiness is social; "man was born for citizenship". It is not pleasure, though pleasure comes as a crown or completion to the activity when it goes right, just as—so Aristotle puts it—physical charm (ὥρα) comes as a completion to youth and health. The motive for good action, however, is not the pleasure that may accompany it; nor yet the happiness which normally does so. When a brave man faces danger or a martyr faces suffering he does so ἕνεκα τοῦ καλοῦ, i.e. literally "for the sake of the beautiful". This phrase gives us modern English a shock. We do not habitually think on these lines, and we have no native English word corresponding to the Greek *kalon*. It does not mean the "showy", nor yet "the artistic". It denotes the sort of action which, as soon as we contemplate it, we admire and love, just as we admire and love a beautiful object, without any thought of personal interest or advantage. The brave man has the choice, let us suppose, of dying for his friends or betraying his friends: as he imagines the two actions he sees that one is "ugly" (αἰσχρόν, the regular Greek word for "base") and the other "beautiful" (καλόν); so he chooses it though it involves pain and death. He may of course be influenced by all sorts of other motives, love of his friends, patriotism, anger, the mere habit of courage, or the like: but the strictly moral motive is preference for the beautiful action over the ugly.

Such *Eudaimonia* implies freedom; a slave can have pleasure, but not *Eudaimonia*. If we consider what kind of "activity of the soul according to virtue" is the highest, most perfect and most characteristic of man as a reasoning animal, it proves to be Contemplation. That is the only activity we can well attribute to God, who must be infinitely blessed and happy. It may be said that, since Reason is not the whole of man but only the highest part, to live entirely in the activity of Reason, i.e. in Contemplation, is a thing too high to aim at. Man is mortal, they tell us, and should have mortal thoughts; but Aristotle, on the contrary, urges that we should "make ourselves as immortal as we can, and strain every nerve to live in accordance with the best thing in us".

Even so we do not escape from material considerations, since even for contemplation, if it is to be good in quality, we need health and leisure. And, after all, in human life, when there are things to be done, the end must be not merely to contemplate but to do. In the practical world, we must try "any way there may be of being good", especially in educating and legislating. And thus we are led straight, and without any change of aim, from the most lofty speculations of ethics to the science of practical politics. Political activity is the conduct of a society seeking *Eudaimonia*, and trying to live according to virtue.

This philosophy, it is easy to see, is civic through and through. It accepts the State as a good thing. It assumes that "Man is born to be a citizen" and is "by nature a social animal". He finds his virtue in performing his civic duty, and only in the service of his community can he become fully "Wise, Temperate, Courageous and Righteous". It is rather a surprise to find that Aristotle was writing at a time when the Greek City State was everywhere failing, and the world being re-shaped on a totally different model by Aristotle's own pupil, Alexander, and his successors. Evidently Aristotle did not regard the system of large military monarchies, backed by a lower civilization, as an improvement on that of the old City States, small, weak and poor, but highly civilized. It is characteristic of Greek democratic feeling that in the whole of Aristotle's works there is no word of flattery to his royal pupil.

6. REVOLT OF THE SOUL AGAINST THE STATE

The School of Aristotle, the Peripatetics, clung firmly for many generations to their master's point of view. But a rebellion of the individual Soul against the State had already begun and was never again without a witness in the Greek world.

It is important, if we would understand the various phases of Greek religion and ethics, to realize it as a philosophy of service, of citizenship, a loyalty of the individual to the whole of which he is a part. There are conditions under which this conception is entirely satisfying. In a ship on a long and stormy voyage the mind of a member of the crew may well be entirely occupied in saving the ship, and the more so the more he loves the ship and admires the captain. This was roughly speaking the position of a good citizen of Athens or Sparta in the early fifth century B.C. But suppose he realizes that his ship is only one of a large fleet; or suppose he thinks that the ship is badly managed or the captain trying to sink her or the object of the voyage slave-trading or piracy? His loyalty will be in different degrees modified or undermined and his duty may become entirely different.

The thought that loyalty must be due not to Athens alone but to all Hellas or all humanity, meets us with increasing frequency from Herodotus onward; the suspicion that the whole government of Athens is incompetent and unjust and, worse still, that her aim in the Great War was tyrannical, is prominent in Euripides, Thucydides and Xenophon. And Plato especially found himself confronted by the paradox of the condemnation of Socrates, in which the City and the Laws, to whom he owed allegiance, were murdering the Just Man because he told them the truth. Plato's answer to the problem is a still more passionate devotion to the State, provided only that the State will be righteous; and, as we have seen, he spent his life in the search for that Righteous City. Isocrates, Xenophon and Lysias in different ways preached a Pan-Hellenic patriotism, as we might to-day preach a Pan-European patriotism, contrasted with the narrow devotion to a man's own city. But in the main philosophy detached itself from earthly patriotisms and, while keeping the ideal of loyalty or social duty, directed it towards some goal at once less limited and less tarnished. Where Aristotle continued to urge the duty of practical "politic", and the importance of studying "what enactments suit what circumstances", most of the other philosophers, despising such worldliness, considered that the proper thing was to pursue "righteousness" or "virtue" as the crow flies, and to know that any City which objected was no true City.

7. ETHICS IN EPICURUS

Two main schools of philosophy arose towards the end of the fourth century and have, in a sense, divided mankind ever since, the Epicurean on the one hand and the Cynic or Stoic on the other. Epicurus was an Athenian of good birth, son of an elementary schoolmaster, who had passed through poverty, defeat in war, exile, bad health and distress in a colony of refugees; had discovered that there is still "sweetness" (ἡδονή) in life; that it can be produced by moderate and temperate living, and that the secret of it lies in not being afraid and in loving one's companions (τὸ θαρρεῖν, φιλία). This "sweetness", sometimes translated "Pleasure", is the Good, or the aim of life. Virtue is only good as a means towards it. Epicurus set to work to free mankind from all their false fears. Why fear death? The dead feel nothing. Why fear the Gods? The Gods cannot harm you. They are blessed beings, and nothing can be blessed which gives pain to another. Why fear pain in this world? Long-continued pain is never intolerable; intense pain is generally brief; a brave man can endure either. He can live the life of the soul, in memory or contemplation, and ignore the petty pains of the present. Next, Epicurus sought to set men free from all the "humbug" of the conventional world. Rank and power and ambition were delusions; better a picnic by a river than all "the crowns of the Greeks". Learning and culture were worthless and deceiving; "From all higher education, my friend, spread sails and fly!" Remember above all that human bliss—"sweetness" or "blessedness", as he sometimes calls it—is not a remote dream but a thing easily won. It is here in your hands, if you will only live temperately, love those about you and not be afraid.

This school was never very numerous. It seems to have owed much to the personality of the founder. Its great work was to liberate the educated Greek world from superstitious terrors. When that work was done its message was largely exhausted, and it was perhaps too modest in its promises and too difficult in its practice to attract multitudes of adherents. Also it suffered deservedly for its founder's contempt for the advance of knowledge. Its two main doctrines, the Atomic Theory in physics, and the Utilitarian Theory in ethics, have come to their kingdom in modern times, but in antiquity the advance of science fell mostly into the hands of the Aristotelians, and the religious struggle against Christianity into those of the Platonists and Stoics. Indeed the pious pagans of the fourth century A.D. were fond of denouncing the Christians and Epicureans together as "atheists".

8. ETHICS OF THE CYNIC AND STOIC SCHOOLS

Yet the Stoics, especially if we couple with them the Cynics from whom they were derived, were largely the source of the moral ideas of Christianity. The difference between Cynic and Stoic seems to have been essentially a difference of education and culture rather than one of doctrine. The Cynics were the Stoics of the slum and the street corner. They were like the Buddhist mendicant monks as compared to the Buddhist philosophers. The first Cynic, Antisthenes, set up his school in a gymnasium appropriated to the use of bastards without citizenship. The most famous, Diogenes, lived like St. Francis in utter poverty, and without even a roof over his head. In later times the Cynic dressed as a beggar, refused all possessions beyond a beggar's staff and wallet, and preached in the streets. It is worth mentioning that women as well as men were found among their preachers, as well as in the quieter ranks of the Stoics and Epicureans; that under the Roman Empire some persons were at the same time Cynic philosophers and Christian monks; and that the abolition of the gladiatorial games was due to the self-sacrificing protest of three persons in succession, two Cynics and the Christian Telemachus. Thus in the Cynic school the transition from the old religion to the new took place almost without a conscious change.

The doctrine of the Cynics was that Virtue ('Ἀρετή, Goodness) was the Good, and nothing else of any worth at all. Virtue was a direct relation of the naked soul to God. Like the Dominicans (Dominicani—"*Domini canes*") after them, the Cynics (κυνικοί, "canine") were the watchdogs of God on earth; like a dog they needed no possessions, no knowledge, no city, only Courage, Temperance, Justice and Wisdom, which consisted in absolute fidelity to the divine Master. The Cynic saint, like the Christian, had affinities not only with the respectable poor, but with sinners and outcasts. Diogenes came to Athens as an ill-mannered young foreigner, whose father, a fraudulent money-changer, had been convicted of "defacing the coinage" and was now in prison. When asked what he wanted in a philosophical school, Diogenes answered: "to deface the coinage". He meant to strip from life all the false stamps and labels put on it by human conventions. He obeyed no human laws, for he recognized no City: he was "citizen of the Cosmos", or universe, and obeyed the laws of God. Through that citizenship he was "free" while all the world was in bondage, "fearless" while others were afraid. He was brother not only to all men, but to the beasts also. When about to die he recommended that his body should be thrown out to the dogs and wolves, who were doubtless hungry. "I should like to be some use to my brothers when I am dead."

He differs from the Stoics and from many of his own followers in having no social message, except the call to repent. Similarly he differed from many leaders of the ancient proletariat, in that he never preached rebellion or attempted to reconstitute society. The most oppressed slave, he considered, had already full access to God and to Virtue, and the greatest king had no more. He did not even correct the possible excesses of his followers by saying, as St. Paul did, "Slaves, obey your masters".

The modern use of the word "cynic" is of course a complete travesty of its original meaning. To most of us the Cynic school seems to suffer not from any lack of idealism, but from an idealism that has run mad through its own narrowness and intensity and its neglect of the secondary values of life. The Stoic school, starting from the same premiss, that "Nothing but Goodness is good", built out of it a system of ethics and—one may fairly say—of religion which, whether one accepts it or not, seems to have a permanent value for mankind. "Nothing but Goodness is good": there is no importance whatever in such things as health or sickness, riches or poverty, pleasure or pain. Who would ever claim credit for such things when his soul stood naked before God? All that matters is the goodness of man's self, that is, of his free and living will. Goodness is to serve the purpose of God, to will what God wills, and thus co-operate with the purpose of the Cosmos. In that spirit Zeno wrote his *Republic*; he conceived a world-society in which there should be no separate States; one great "City of gods and men", where all should be citizens and members one of another, bound together not by human laws but by Love.

In the world as a whole, then, there is a purpose, and Virtue, or Goodness, is co-operation with that purpose. It was easier then than it is now to see a purpose revealed in the discoveries of science. For science had in the fourth century just reached a conception of the world which was singularly satisfying to the human mind. Astronomy had shown that the heavenly bodies followed perfectly regular movements. The stars were no wandering fires, but parts of an immense and eternal order. And though this order in its fullness might remain inscrutable, its main essence at least could be divined from the fact—then accepted as certain—that the orbits of all the celestial bodies had for their centre our earth and its ephemeral master, Man. Whatever else the Purpose might be, it was the purpose of a God who loves Man and has placed him in the centre of the Universe.

Add to this the conception of Nature which the Stoics had learned from Aristotle and others, as a system of Phusis or "growth" towards perfection—of the seed towards the oak, of the blind puppy towards the good hound, of the primeval savage towards the civilized man—and one can see how this "*Phusis*" becomes identical with the Forethought or "*providentia*" of God. The whole movement of the Cosmos is the fulfilment of God's will. Virtue is action harmonious with that will; wickedness, the attempt to assert one's own contemptible will against it, an attempt which besides being blasphemous must always be futile. This line of thought ends in a paradox or an apparent contradiction, sublime and perhaps insoluble, which is common to Stoicism and Christianity. We recognize that in this great Cosmos or Order each living creature has its part. It is the part of the deer to grow swifter and stronger; of the artist to produce beauty; of the governor to govern well, so as to produce a prosperous and well-ordered city. At the same time we must remember that none of these things at which we aim, speed, beauty, prosperity or the like, are of any real value in themselves; nothing matters at all except the Good Will, the willing fulfilment of the Purpose of God. It does not really matter if all our efforts in this world are defeated. It is His will that we should strive, it may not be His will that we should succeed. We must not be too bitterly disappointed. If our friends die and we suffer great sorrows we may groan; that is human and pardonable. But ἔσωθεν, in the centre of our being, we must not groan. We must accept the eternal purpose and be content, though we perish.

Most adherents of evolutionist or "meliorist" systems fall into the speculatively unsound position of justifying the present by the future. Imperfect man is so constantly preoccupied with the morrow, and so well content if he can see the labour and discomfort of the present repaid by success hereafter, that he is apt to transfer the same conception to the divine and perfect scheme. The world may be a miserable place now; that does not matter, he argues, if it is going to be a happy place hereafter. He sees no difficulty in supposing that the purpose of God, like that of a man, may be thwarted for a long time as long as it is ultimately triumphant. The conception seems clearly to be unsound. Even in human action one would feel some compunction about a plan which condemned a number of individuals to misery in order that after their death some other people should be happy. The Stoics at any rate were firm against any such lines of thought. Virtue is the good now; the Purpose is being fulfilled now; the Cosmos is infinitely beautiful now—now and always. They entirely refuse to promise future rewards to Virtue or to justify the present injustices of the world by the prospect of a millennium. The sufferings are of no importance: the only thing that matters is the way in which we face them.

The special advantage of Stoicism over most other systems is that, like Christianity, it adapts itself equally to a world order which we accept as good or to one which we reject as evil. Though it originated in a rebellion of the soul against society, it can equally well become a religion of social service. Many of the Hellenistic kings and great Roman governors were Stoics. Some of the great revolutionary reformers were inspired by Stoic advisers. Stoicism taught them to fulfil the divine purpose by governing as well and justly as they could, while at the same time it afforded a theoretical comfort if their efforts failed. Consequently it held its own both in the good periods and the bad. It comforted Brutus and Cato in the death agonies of the Roman republic; it fortified the lame slave Epictetus;

it inspired the good Emperor, Marcus Aurelius, in his care for a peaceful and well-administered world. Doubtless it tended at times to protest too much; to try to solve the riddles of life by sententious preaching and rhetorical paradoxes, as in Seneca; but it never compromised its lofty spirit and never sank into vulgar superstition or emotionalism.

9. THE "FAILURE OF NERVE": MYSTICISM AND SUPERSTITION

But we must realize that there was plenty of superstition and emotionalism about. It hardly appears in the classical writers who have come down to us, and we are tempted to think it was not there. But the evidence is abundant. We do not need the testimony of Epicurus, Lucretius, the early Christian fathers, or Theophrastus in his account of "The Superstitious Man", to show the prevalence and strength of superstition. It is shown by many incidents in history, and brought home by the religious inscriptions, the rites recorded by the antiquarian Pausanias, the fragments of mystical and magical literature. And there seems now to be evidence to show that the kind of conception which has hitherto been supposed to be characteristic of the decadence of the Hellenic world was really present in pre-Hellenic Crete. (See Evans in *J.H.S.*, vol. XLV,

"The Ring of Nestor".) There is no cause for surprise in this. Many words which occur in Homer disappeared in classical Greek only to re-emerge in late Ptolemaic papyri or in modern speech. The common people, in Greece as elsewhere, went on comparatively unaffected by the great spiritual and intellectual movements of Hellenism. Socrates or the Stoics might preach, Epicurus might disprove, but the Boeotian peasant went on placating the same old bogies in the same old way as his remote ancestors. And it is notable how the various periods of economic distress or prolonged warfare which fell upon the Greek world brought about a decline of culture and a revival of primitive beliefs.

Men are apt to regard their misfortunes as the punishment of unforgiven sins. The famous earthquake of Lisbon was expiated by the burning of a large number of Jews: the eruption of Mont Pélée in our own day was followed by great public ceremonies of repentance. Greece was the home, from pre-Hellenic times, of rites of initiation or mysteries, such as exist in many barbarous tribes at the present day. In their simplest form these rites formed the initiation of the boys of the tribe into manhood, and the exposition to them of certain secret truths or doctrines that only the grown men of the tribe might know. But in practice we find that, as tribes disappeared or turned into voluntary societies, the rites began to have a different meaning. They brought purification from sin or pollution; they brought the communicant into close relation with some mediating god and gave him some assurance of bliss in the next world. Those who were not initiated, and thus accepted into the community of the faithful, would remain outcast from bliss. Plato and other writers are scornful of these doctrines and the votaries who live by them, professing to "forgive sins" and secure that an initiated thief would fare better in the next world than an uninitiated just man. But the doctrines lived and spread.

For similar reasons, perhaps, there had early been a religion of the "Sôtêr", the Saviour or Deliverer. Sometimes it is a mere title, as in "Zeus Sôtêr": sometimes it is "the Saviour" alone, or more especially "The Third, the Saviour", or "the Saviour who is Third" ($\tau\rho\acute{\iota}\tau o\varsigma$ $\Sigma\omega\tau\acute{\eta}\rho$). The origin of this conception seems probably to lie in the old agricultural religion which created and worshipped so many beings to represent the Year, or the Season, or the Vegetation, gods whose coming was the coming of spring or else of harvest, and whose annual death was celebrated when the harvest was cut or the vegetation died. The God had been killed—most often torn in pieces and scattered over the fields—by a second Being, his Enemy, through whose victory the life of the earth seemed dead, till there came a Third Being, a Saviour, who slew the Enemy and brought back the dead God, or was himself the dead God restored. Modern travellers have found remains of this worship in modern Greece, and something like it continues in many parts of Europe.

In Hellenistic times, and particularly in the terrible times of strain that came between the Punic Wars and the Battle of Actium, this Saviour religion took a more spiritual or mystical character. It was associated with many names from the old mythology or from new Oriental systems, from the old Heracles to the new Isis and Sarapis, or the compound Hermes-Thoth. Notably Asclepius, the divine physician, not previously a god of much importance outside his temple at Epidaurus, became for some generations the most passionately worshipped god in the eastern Mediterranean. The world was sick, and cried out for the Healer.

In some of the earliest and most primitive rituals the climax of ecstatic worship was to bring the worshipper into "communion", to make him one with his God. The communion originally involved drinking the blood and eating the flesh of the god, though in some of the sects called "Gnostic" it came through ecstasy and contemplation. For to "know" God, in this context, meant to be made one with him. ($\Gamma\nu\hat{\omega}\sigma\iota\varsigma$ = knowledge.) The Gnostic writings have come down to us mixed up with later additions from many sources, and it is hard to separate out the original pre-Christian doctrines. But the Saviour seems generally to be a "Third", the other two being God the Father and some such being as the Divine "Wisdom" (Sophia) or "Spirit". (In some sects the second person is still the Enemy, as in the old Year-Daemon rituals, and "the god of the Jews" made into a kind of Satan.) The method of redemption is sometimes that of the dying or suffering God, as he appears in the oldest agricultural religions; sometimes that of the "righteous man" in Plato, who is happy though he be condemned of men and in the end impaled or crucified. Meantime the old ideas of astrology newly imported from Babylon have run riot through Greek thought, and the Saviour descends, by his own will or that of the Father, through all the spheres of the sinister Seven Planets, who rule the earth, to save mankind, or it may be to re-awaken in man the Soul, or the divine Sophia or Wisdom, who has forgotten her true nature.

Many details might be added to illustrate the various forms taken by these Saviour Religions, and the curious and often beautiful speculations which they engendered. But the main root of them seems to be a feeling of disillusion or despair of the world; the feeling of men in the presence of forces which they can neither control nor understand. They cry to their new God because the old gods have failed and there is none other to hear or help them. They seek to be saved not by "justice" or wise conduct, but by some act of sacrifice or purification, some intensity of adoration. The forms and theories are merely those which happen to be supplied by old tradition or by the customs of some foreign hierophant, coming perhaps from Egypt or Babylon.

10. MITHRAISM

Historically the most important of these religious communities, at once the nearest and the most hostile to Christianity, came not from the Levant but from higher and remoter regions of the East. There were worshippers of Mithras in extreme antiquity, before the ancestors of the Persians separated from those of the Hindoos. Even under the Roman Empire they liked to worship in caves, as they had before temples existed, and drew their myths and parables from pastoral life, as it had been before the building of cities. Of old Mithras had been a high God; but now he had lost in rank and gained in vitality. He was a hero, a redeemer, a mediator between man and god, a champion ever armed and vigilant in the eternal war of Ormuzd against Ahriman, of light against evil and darkness.

This religion hardly touched Greece at all. The severe Iranian dualism held out almost as rigorously as did the monotheism of the Jews against the general hellenization which followed the conquests of Alexander. There are no Greek names derived from Mithras, as there are none from Jehovah, though "Isidotus", "Serapion", etc., are fairly common. Mithraism is said to have come to Rome from Cilicia and Pontus, after the campaign of Pompeius against the pirates and the rebel King Mithridates (65–61 B.C.). From thence onward it was carried by a stream of slaves and captives to Rome and the Mediterranean ports, and still more by a stream of soldiers out to the legions. Mithraism stretched at this time from Persia to the Euxine Sea, and covered some of the best recruiting-grounds. It spread along all the frontiers of the Empire, especially on the east and north, where life was most dangerous.

It was the religion of an unconquered people, the religion for a man and a soldier, not like Christianity, a doctrine for the conquered and subject. It had no place for the emotional women who swarmed in the Oriental cults and had a considerable influence in Christianity. We hear of no priestesses or female initiates: only of virgins, to share the worship of a virgin soldiery. It was in many ways more like an order of chivalry than a religious sect. There were ascetic vows, and an organized self-denial. The Mithraic might accept no earthly crown: "His crown was Mithras". There were rites of baptism and confirmation; but the confirmation was preceded by stern ordeals, and the baptism was not a dipping in water but a branding with hot iron. The adherent of Mithras was throughout life a warrior, fighting for Ormuzd, for the Light, for the Sun, as against all that was dark and unclean. Since Mithras was "The Sun, the Unconquered", and the Sun was "the royal Star", the religion looked for a King whom it could serve as the representative of Mithras upon earth: and since the proof that the "Grace" of Ormuzd rested upon a king was, of course, in addition to his virtue and piety, his invincibility, the Roman Emperor seemed to be clearly indicated as the true King. In sharp contrast to Christianity, Mithraism recognized Caesar as the bearer of the divine Grace, and its votaries filled the legions and the civil service.

Yet the similarities between Mithraism and Christianity are striking, and may be taken as signs of the spiritual and psychological needs of the time. Mithraism arose in the East, among the poor, among captives and slaves. It put its hopes in a Redeemer, a Mediator, who performed some mystical sacrifice. It held a Communion Service of bread and wine. It rested on the personal *Pistis* (Faith, or faithfulness) of the convert to his Redeemer. It had so much acceptance that it was able to impose on the Christian world its own Sun-Day in place of the Sabbath; its Sun's birthday, December 25, as the birthday of Jesus; its Magi and its Shepherds hailing the divine Star; and various of its Easter Celebrations.

On the other hand, its Redeemer, Mithras, makes hardly any pretence to have had an earthly history. His saga is all myth and allegory, elaborate ritual, sacraments and mystic names, and the varied paraphrasing that is necessary for bringing primitive superstitions up to the level which civilized man will tolerate. Above all, it differed from Christianity in that, having made its peace with Rome, it accepted not only the Empire but the other religions of the Empire. Rome saw in the second century the usefulness of Mithraism, and the Emperor Commodus was initiated: Mithraism became inextricably involved in the other Sun worships as well as those of Isis and the Great Mother, and thus sank into the slough of turbid syncretism in which the

Empire of Septimius Severus and Elagabalus tried to find a universal religion.

Mithraism must have lost much of its purity and vigour before it met its great military disaster. In the Dacian Revolt of A.D. 257, following on the Gothic invasions, Mithras proved too weak to withstand the barbarians. He was no longer "The Unconquered". His cave-chapels, or Mithraea, were destroyed all along the frontier where they had been at their strongest. The sect never recovered. Doubtless they had encouraged persecution of the Christians in previous times, and now the Christians had their chance. The little chapels, never with a congregation of more than a hundred, were a fairly easy prey to large mobs. A candidate for Christian baptism in St. Jerome's letters offers as a proof of his piety his exploits in wrecking them. Excavations of the Mithraea, which are exceedingly numerous all over the imperial frontiers, show sometimes how the priests had walled them up, with the holy objects inside, in the hope of reopening the worship in better days; sometimes how the Christian mobs had polluted them for ever with the rotting corpses of the faithful. A bloody and cruel story, like so much of the history of religion; but it is clear that Christianity gained in strength by defying the Roman world longer than Mithras did, and by denying instead of accepting its numerous gods.

11. WHAT THE AGE NEEDED

A study of the Gnostic and Hermetic collections, and such evidence as exists about the worships of Isis, Serapis, Mithras and various Saviours, together with the magical remains and the accounts of early heresies, leaves on the mind the impression of a mass of emotional and spiritual aspiration, marred by nervous and intellectual wreckage. The world passed through a bad period after the Second Punic War, and another in the troubles of the third century A.D. and then in the final fall, but it is difficult to assign dates to movements of which one does not know the local or social origin. The mystic literature as a whole bears a message of despair and consolation—despair of living a good life by one's own efforts in so unrighteous a world, and consolation by promises of ultimate reward whose extreme splendour makes up for their regrettable uncertainty. Here and there the future bliss for ourselves is crossed by a vision of the well-deserved torments that await our enemies and persecutors. It is the cry of the failure of the old Graeco-Roman civilization, though of course that failure may have been felt in different degrees at very different places and dates.

It seems clear that any new religion which was to have a chance of success at this time must be one that appealed to the ignorant masses—though no doubt it would be a great advantage if it were capable also, like Stoicism, of being adapted to the needs of the philosophers. It must promise a personal salvation by the active help of a personal god, who must also be as solid and human as possible. A god who was pure thought "without body, parts or passions" would be of no avail. It must be a religion of the poor, though whether the rich should be given their deserts now or left to receive them in hell was a point which depended upon circumstances. (In 130 B.C., when suffering was intense, the madder alternative had been tried with disastrous results; in the first century of the Empire there was peace and good government, and consequently far less suffering and more meekness.) It must in the main satisfy man's moral nature, for the present discontent was not merely due to personal suffering but also to a rage against the injustice of the world and a feeling that such misery must somehow be the result of sin. Lastly, it must clearly profess doctrines which were natural and acceptable to the masses of the Mediterranean world; that is, it must be based on the old religions. At the same time it could not belong to one nation only, but must have some wider appeal, the old familiar emotion being stimulated by the new revelation. Thus the Hermetic system is derived from Greece and Egypt, Mithraism from Iran and Babylon with a touch of Hellenism, Christianity from Greece and Judaism.

Whether Christianity is to be explained as a natural development from the existing factors, or whether it is a miraculous revelation vouchsafed after long delay to a world that had been allowed to grow exactly ripe for it, is a problem which cannot be settled by historical research and must be answered by each man according to his own bent. But it is curious how all the main articles of Christian faith and practice were already latent in the ancient religion. The parts of Christian doctrine which a Levantine pagan of the first century would deny are chiefly the historical statements. Like Paul before his conversion, he would be ready enough to discuss the doctrine of a Hebrew Messiah or a Hellenistic "Saviour", but would refuse to believe that this supernatural being had just arrived on earth in the person of a certain Jew or Nazarene. He would feel no surprise at the moral teaching; he would have met parts of it in the Jewish tradition and parts in Stoicism. At worst he might be alarmed at the revolutionary tone of certain parts and the exaltation of one who was, after all, a condemned criminal, as the ideal good man and Son of God. The rejection of bloody sacrifice he had learnt from the Peripatetics and the Jews; conceptions like the Good Shepherd, the Mother and Child, the worship of a divine Baby, the halo round the heads of saints, and innumerable other incidents of Christian tradition, were of course not new inventions but things ancient and familiar. The transition consisted largely in giving a new name and history to some object of worship which already had had many names and varying legends attached to it. Nay more, in the metaphysical and theological doctrines formulated in the Creeds, except where they were specially meant to controvert the old system, he would at least recognize for the most part ideas which he had heard discussed.

12. THE CREEDS, CHRISTIAN AND PAGAN: THE AREA OF AGREEMENT

He believed in God as a "Father" and would have no quarrel with a Christian as to the exact meaning of that metaphorical term; the attribute "Almighty" he accepted, though both Christian and pagan theologians had the same difficulty in dealing with the implications of that term and explaining how the All-good and Almighty permitted evil. The average Greek did not think of God as the "maker of heaven and earth"; the thought was Hebrew or Babylonian, but was not strange to the Hellenistic world. The idea of an "only-begotten Son" of God was regular in the Orphic systems, and that of a Son of God by a mortal woman, conceived in some spiritual way, and born for the saving of mankind, was at least as old as the fifth century B.C. In a simpler and more natural form it was much earlier. That this Saviour "suffered and was buried" is common to the Vegetation or Year religions, with their dying and suffering gods; and the idea had been sharpened and made more living both by the thought of Plato's "righteous man" and by the various "kings of the Poor" who had risen and suffered in the slave revolts. That after the descent to Hades he should arise to judge both the quick and the dead is a slight modification of the ordinary Greek notion, according to which the Judges were already seated at their work, but it may have come from the Saviour religions.

The belief in God as a Trinity, or as One substance with three "*personae*"—the word simply means "masks" or "dramatic roles"—is directly inherited from Greek speculation. The third person was more usually feminine, the divine Wisdom, or Providence, or the Mother of the Son: the "Spirit" or "Breath of God" comes from the Hebrew. Belief in the Holy Catholic Church was again not the pagan's own belief, but it was the sort of belief with which he was quite familiar. He accepted belief in some church or community, be it that of Mithras or Hermes-Thoth or some similar Healer. If the "communion of the Saints" originally meant the sharing of all property among the faithful, that practice was familiar in certain congregations; if it meant, as is now generally understood, the existence of a certain fellowship or community between those who are "pure", whether dead, living, or divine, it was an idea prevalent in Stoicism. The "forgiveness of sins" was a subject much debated in antiquity as at the time of the Reformation. The traditional religion dealt largely in "purification", which involved forgiveness of sins and slipped from time to time into a mechanical or mercenary treatment of the matter, which roused the usual protest of indignation and denial. It is interesting also to note that a closely cognate idea, the "forgiveness of debts", was one of the regular cries of the proletarian movements. A connection was probably felt between a generous Leader—like Cleomenes III or C. Gracchus—who annulled poor men's debts on earth and a God who forgave them their offences in heaven. Of the Resurrection of the body we have already spoken; it was a concession to the uneducated, who would not be content with a "life everlasting" of the soul alone, freed from bodily substance and form, and perhaps even from personality.

The greatest blot upon Christianity was the savage emphasis which it laid upon the doctrine of Hell—and that a Hell specially reserved, not so much for the wicked, but for all those who did not belong to the Christian community. Yet here also there is nothing absolutely new. Mithras and Isis and even the God of Neoplatonism tolerated some tormenting demons. And after all Hell for the persecutor in the next life is the natural retort of the victim who cannot hit back in this life. One may well imagine that the followers of Spartacus, Aristonicus or Mithridates believed in a Hell for Romans. And the peculiar notion of treating false belief as a form of sin, and a particularly dangerous form, goes back to the wise and gentle Plato himself.[1]

In the same way, if we compare briefly with the Christian Creeds the document drawn up by Sallustius for the education of the young pagans in religion, we shall not find much that a modern Christian would care to deny, though we shall notice how much more intellectual, abstract, and in a sense aristocratic, is the doctrine of the Neoplatonist.

[1] *Laws*, p. 908.

The young are to be thoroughly trained in the knowledge that God is free from passion and change, eternal, unbegotten, incorporeal, not in time or space. He is good and the cause of good; He is never angry nor appeased. (Much of this would clash vividly with parts of the Hebrew and Christian story but not much with modern theology.) They are to know that the ancient myths are all allegories; they mean not what they say, but reveal hidden wisdom. (This is the usual refuge of a society which has outgrown its sacred book.) The Cosmos is eternal and can never come to an end. (The Christians, of course, were eagerly expecting the end of it.) The first Cause is the Good; i.e. all things throughout the Cosmos move from love of the Good, though as a rule they do not know it: there is no positive evil, and of course no evil caused by God. The soul is immortal; human freedom, Divine Providence, Fate and Fortune have all their place and can be reconciled. Virtue consists in four parts, Wisdom, Courage, Temperance, Righteousness. Men worship God, not to benefit Him or show honour to Him; for of course we cannot affect Him in any way. We merely rejoice in Him as we rejoice in the beauty of the Sun. Similarly those who deny or reject God (i.e. the Christians and Epicureans) do Him no injury; they are like men in the sunlight who cannot see the Sun, either because they are blind or because they insist on looking away from it. Goodness is not a painful thing to be rewarded by future bliss; it is blessedness both now and hereafter.

13. CHRISTIANITY ON THE SIDE OF PROGRESS

It is difficult at this distance of time to form any judgement about the comparative morals of the early Christian communities and the pagan societies in which they lived. We may indeed be fairly sure that the average mass of sensual men, with their commonplace vices and dishonesties, did not trouble to become Christian before Constantine made it the easier course, nor dare to stay pagan afterwards. The polemical writings of the Christians are preserved, those of the pagans have mostly perished; but we can see that the lurid accusations hurled by each against their opponents are nearly all based on what is called constructive evidence. The pagans argue that people who deny the gods, who worship a condemned criminal, and who pray that the whole world may soon be destroyed, must be inconceivably wicked and malignant; the Christians, that people whose mythical gods committed adultery and cannibalism, must themselves be ready for any enormity. Such accusations are like the stories circulated about Jews and Anabaptists in the Middle Ages. They are only symptoms of the accusers' state of mind, not evidence against the accused.

In general we must remember that the Christians belonged mostly to the seething town proletariate of the eastern Mediterranean; the pagans, as that name implies, seem to have been the unprogressive peasants of the country villages (*pagi*), though the word has a secondary meaning, "civilian", and may have been intended to denote the common herd as distinct from the soldiers of Mithras or Christ. One can easily understand how the excesses of the town mobs would be attributed by the timid respectable classes to the terrible inroads of Christianity. But the mob was really neither pagan nor Christian. The idealists, rebels, reformers, among the working class, would be mostly either Christians or followers of some other mystic sect, though the more intellectual might become philosophers. The Jewish element in Christianity, also, was a separating influence and made for a higher morality. The Jews uncompromisingly denounced certain practices, notably homosexuality and abortion, which the world as a whole tolerated and only philosophers and certain special communities condemned. The crusade against the lusts of the flesh which marked the centuries just before and after the Christian era was by no means specially Christian, though doubtless here as elsewhere Christianity was against the dead mass and for the reforming few.

But there is certainly one point in which Christianity, at any rate in its earlier forms, did a unique service to the world. In its rejection of superstition it stands far higher than the rival religions, higher even than the Neoplatonism of Proclus and Julian, infinitely higher than the paganism of the vulgar. When Julian condemns the Christians as "atheists" or "rejectors of God" he is giving them the highest praise. The beautiful dialogue *Octavius*, attributed to Minucius Felix, shows how, to an educated man, Christianity came as a liberation from the perpetual presence of objects of superstitious worship. It performed the same cleansing task as Judaic monotheism among the worshippers of the Baalim, as Islam among the Arabian pagans, and as one side at least of the Reformation. The ancient world, as civilization declined, was overburdened by the ever-increasing mass of its superstitions, and its thought devitalized by a blind reverence for the past. Philosophy as well as religion could hardly find life except through a process of which the first step was a vigorous denial of false gods. That step once taken, it is curious to observe how little of ancient philosophy has perished, how much has merely been taken over by Christianity, and how few new ideas in the realms of metaphysics or morals have occurred to the human mind since the fourth century before Christ.

II

The Stoic Philosophy

II

THE STOIC PHILOSOPHY

I PROPOSE to give here in rough outline some
account of the greatest system of organized
thought which the mind of man had built up
for itself in the Graeco-Roman world before the
coming of Christianity with its inspired book
and its authoritative revelation. Stoicism may be
called either a philosophy or a religion. It was
a religion in its exalted passion; it was a philosophy inasmuch as it made no pretence to magical powers or supernatural knowledge. I do not
suggest that it is a perfect system, with no errors
of fact and no inconsistencies of theory. It is
certainly not that; and I do not know of any
system that is. But I believe that it represents a
way of looking at the world and the practical
problems of life which possesses still a permanent
interest for the human race, and a permanent
power of inspiration. I shall approach it, therefore, rather as a psychologist than as a philosopher
or historian. I shall not attempt to trace the
growth or variation of Stoic doctrine under its
various professors, nor yet to scrutinize the

logical validity of its arguments. I shall merely try as best I can to make intelligible its great central principles and the almost irresistible appeal which they made to so many of the best minds of antiquity.

From this point of view I will begin by a very rough general suggestion—viz. that the religions known to history fall into two broad classes, religions which are suited for times of good government and religions which are suited for times of bad government; religions for prosperity or for adversity, religions which accept the world or which defy the world, which place their hopes in the betterment of human life on this earth or which look away from it as from a vale of tears. By "the world" in this connection I mean the ordinary concrete world, the well-known companion of the flesh and the Devil; not the universe. For some of the religions which think most meanly of the world they know have a profound admiration for all, or nearly all, those parts of the universe where they have not been.

Now, to be really successful in the struggle for existence, a religion must suit both sets of circumstances. A religion which fails in adversity, which deserts you just when the world deserts you, would be a very poor affair; on the other hand, it is almost equally fatal for a religion to collapse as soon as it is successful. Stoicism, like Christianity, was primarily a religion for the oppressed, a religion of defence and defiance; but, like Christianity, it had the requisite power of adaptation. Consistently or inconsistently, it opened its wings to embrace the needs both of success and of failure. To illustrate what I mean —contrast for the moment the life of an active, practical, philanthropic, modern Bishop with that of an anchorite like St. Simeon Stylites, living in idleness and filth on the top of a large column; or, again, contrast the Bishop's ideals with those of the author of the Apocalypse, abandoning himself to visions of a gorgeous reversal of the order of this evil world and the bloody revenges of the blessed. All three are devout Christians; but the Bishop is working with the world of men, seeking its welfare and helping its practical needs; the other two are rejecting or cursing it. In somewhat the same way we shall find that our two chief preachers of Stoicism are, the one a lame and penniless slave to whom worldly success is as nothing, the other an Emperor of Rome, keenly interested in good administration.

The founder of the Stoic school, Zeno, came from Cilicia to Athens about the year 320 B.C. His place of birth is, perhaps, significant. He was a Semite, and came from the East. The

Semite was apt in his religion to be fierier and more uncompromising than the Greek. The time of his coming is certainly significant. It was a time when landmarks had collapsed, and human life was left, as it seemed, without a guide. The average man in Greece of the fifth century B.C. had two main guides and sanctions for his conduct of life: the welfare of his City and the laws and traditions of his ancestors. First the City, and next the traditional religion; and in the fourth century both of these had fallen. Let us see how.

Devotion to the City or Community produced a religion of public service. The City represented a high ideal, and it represented supreme power. By 320 B.C. the supreme power had been overthrown. Athens, and all independent Greek cities, had fallen before the overwhelming force of the great military monarchies of Alexander and his generals. The high ideal at the same time was seen to be narrow. The community to which a man should devote himself, if he should devote himself at all, must surely be something larger than one of these walled cities set upon their separate hills. Thus the City, as a guide of life, had proved wanting. Now when the Jews lost their Holy City they had still, or believed that they had still, a guide left. "Zion is taken from us," says the Book of Esdras; "nothing is left save the Holy One and His Law". But Greece had no such Law. The Greek religious tradition had long since been riddled with criticism. It would not bear thinking out, and the Greeks liked to think things out. The traditional religion fell not because the people were degenerate. Quite the contrary; it fell, as it has sometimes fallen elsewhere, because the people were progressive. The people had advanced, and the traditional religion had not kept pace with them. And we may add another consideration. If the Gods of tradition had proved themselves capable of protecting their worshippers, doubtless their many moral and intellectual deficiencies might have been overlooked. But they had not. They had proved no match for Alexander and the Macedonian phalanx.

Thus the work that lay before the generation of 320 B.C. was twofold. They had to rebuild a new public spirit, devoted not to the City, but to something greater; and they had to rebuild a religion or philosophy which should be a safe guide in the threatening chaos. We will see how Zeno girded himself to this task.

Two questions lay before him—how to live and what to believe. His real interest was in the first, but it could not be answered without first facing the second. For if we do not in the least know what is true or untrue, real or unreal, we cannot form any reliable rules about conduct or anything else. And, as it happened, the Sceptical school of philosophy, largely helped by Plato, had lately been active in denying the possibility of human knowledge and throwing doubt on the very existence of reality. Their arguments were extraordinarily good, and many of them have not been answered yet; they affect both the credibility of the senses and the supposed laws of reasoning. The Sceptics showed how the senses are notoriously fallible and contradictory, and how the laws of reasoning lead by equally correct processes to opposite conclusions. Many modern philosophers, from Kant to Dr. Schiller and Mr. Bertrand Russell, have followed respectfully in their footsteps. But Zeno had no patience with this sort of thing. He wanted to get to business.

Also he was a born fighter. His dealings with opponents who argued against him always remind me of a story told of the Duke of Wellington when his word was doubted by a subaltern. The Duke, when he was very old and incredibly distinguished, was telling how once, at mess in the Peninsula, his servant had opened a bottle of port, and inside found a rat. "It must have been a very large bottle", remarked the subaltern. The Duke fixed him with his eye. "It was a damned small bottle." "Oh", said the subaltern, abashed; "then no doubt it was a very small rat". "It was a damned large rat", said the Duke. And there the matter has rested ever since.

Zeno began by asserting the existence of the real world. "What do you mean by real?" asked the Sceptic. "I mean solid and material. I mean that this table is solid matter." "And God", said the Sceptic, "and the soul? Are they solid matter?" "Perfectly solid," says Zeno; "more solid, if anything, than the table." "And virtue or justice or the Rule of Three; also solid matter?" "Of course," said Zeno; "quite solid." This is what may be called "high doctrine", and Zeno's successors eventually explained that their master did not really mean that justice was solid matter, but that it was a sort of "tension", or mutual relation, among material objects. This amendment saves the whole situation. But it is well to remember the uncompromising materialism from which the Stoic system started.

Now we can get a step further. If the world is real, how do we know about it? By the evidence of our senses; for the sense-impression (here Stoics and Epicureans both followed the fifth-century physicists) is simply the imprint of the real thing upon our mind-stuff. As such it must be true. In the few exceptional cases where we say that "our senses deceive us" we speak incorrectly. The sense-impression was all right;

it is we who have interpreted it wrongly, or received it in some incomplete way. What we need in each case is a "comprehensive sense-impression". The meaning of this phrase is not quite clear. I think it means a sense-impression which "grasps" its object; but it may be one which "grasps" us, or which we "grasp", so that we cannot doubt it. In any case, when we get the real imprint of the object upon our senses, then this imprint is of necessity true. When the Sceptics talk about a conjuror making "our senses deceive us", or when they object that a straight stick put half under water looks as if it were bent in the middle, they are talking inexactly. In such cases the impression is perfectly true; it is the interpretation that may go wrong. Similarly, when they argue that reasoning is fallacious because men habitually make mistakes in it, they are confusing the laws of reasoning with the inexact use which people make of them. You might just as well say that twice two is not four, or that 7×7 is not 49, because people often make mistakes in doing arithmetic.

Thus we obtain a world which is in the first place real and in the second knowable. Now we can get to work on our real philosophy, our doctrine of ethics and conduct. And we build it upon a very simple principle, laid down first by Zeno's master, Crates, the founder of the Cynic

School: the principle that Nothing but Goodness is Good. That seems plain enough, and harmless enough; and so does its corollary: "Nothing but badness is bad". In the case of any concrete object which you call "good", it seems quite clear that it is only good because of some goodness in it. We, perhaps, should not express the matter in quite this way, but we should scarcely think it worth while to object if Zeno chooses to phrase it so, especially as the statement itself seems little better than a truism.

Now, to an ancient Greek the form of the phrase was quite familiar. He was accustomed to asking "What is the good?" It was to him the central problem of conduct. It meant: "What is the object of life, or the element in things which makes them worth having?" Thus the principle will mean: "Nothing is worth living for except goodness". The only good for man is to *be* good. And, as we might expect, when Zeno says "good" he means good in an ultimate Day-of-Judgement sense, and will take no half-measures. The principle turns out to be not nearly so harmless as it looked. It begins by making a clean sweep of the ordinary conventions. You remember the eighteenth-century lady's epitaph which ends: "Bland, passionate, and deeply religious, she was second cousin to the Earl of Leitrim, and of such are the kingdom of heaven". One doubts whether, when the critical moment came, her relationships would really prove as important as her executors hoped; and it is the same with all the conventional goods of the world when brought before the bar of Zeno. Rank, riches, social distinction, health, pleasure, barriers of race or nation—what will those things matter before the tribunal of ultimate truth? Not a jot. Nothing but goodness is good. It is what you are that matters—what you yourself are; and all these things are not you. They are external; they depend not on you alone, but on other people. The thing that really matters depends on you, and on none but you. From this there flows a very important and surprising conclusion. You possess already, if you only knew it, all that is worth desiring. The good is yours if you but will it. You need fear nothing. You are safe, inviolable, utterly free. A wicked man or an accident can cause you pain, break your leg, make you ill; but no earthly power can make you good or bad except yourself, and to be good or bad is the only thing that matters.

At this point common sense rebels. The plain man says to Zeno: "This is all very well; but we know as a matter of fact that such things as health, pleasure, long life, fame, etc., are good; we all like them. The reverse are bad; we hate and avoid them. All sane, healthy people agree in judging so." Zeno's answer is interesting. In the first place, he says: "Yes; that is what most people say. But the judges who give that judgement are bribed. Pleasure, though not really good, has just that particular power of bribing the judges, and making them on each occasion say or believe that she is good. The Assyrian king Sardanapalus thinks it good to stay in his harem, feasting and merry-making, rather than suffer hardship in governing his kingdom. He swears his pleasure is good; but what will any unbribed third person say? Consider the judgements of history. Do you ever find that history praises a man because he was healthy, or long-lived, or because he enjoyed himself a great deal? History never thinks of such things; they are valueless and disappear from the world's memory. The thing that lives is a man's goodness, his great deeds, his virtue, or his heroism."

If the questioner was not quite satisfied, Zeno used another argument. He would bid him answer honestly for himself: "Would you yourself really like to be rich and corrupted? To have abundance of pleasure and be a worse man?" And, apparently, when Zeno's eyes were upon you, it was difficult to say you would. Some Stoics took a particular instance. When Harmodius and Aristogeiton, the liberators of Athens, slew the tyrant Hipparchus (which is always taken as a praiseworthy act), the tyrant's friends seized a certain young girl, named Leaina, who was the mistress of Aristogeiton, and tortured her to make her divulge the names of the conspirators. And under the torture the girl bit out her tongue and died without speaking a word. Now, in her previous life we may assume that Leaina had had a good deal of gaiety. Which would you sooner have as your own—the early life of Leaina, which was full of pleasures, or the last hours of Leaina, which were full of agony? And with a Stoic's eyes upon them, as before, people found it hard to say the first. They yielded their arms and confessed that goodness, and not any kind of pleasure, is the good.

But now comes an important question, and the answer to it, I will venture to suggest, just redeems Stoicism from the danger of becoming one of those inhuman cast-iron systems by which mankind may be browbeaten, but against which it secretly rebels. What *is* Goodness? What is this thing which is the only object worth living for?

Zeno seems to have been a little impatient of the question. We know quite well; everybody knows who is not blinded by passion or desire. Still, the school consented to analyse it. And the profound common sense and reasonableness of average Greek thought expressed the answer in its own characteristic way. Let us see in practice what we mean by "good". Take a good bootmaker, a good father, a good musician, a good horse, a good chisel; you will find that each one of them has some function to perform, some special work to do; and a good one does the work well. Goodness is performing your function well. But when we say "well" we are still using the idea of goodness. What do we mean by doing it "well"? Here the Greek falls back on a scientific conception which had great influence in the fifth century B.C., and, somewhat transformed and differently named, has regained it in our own days. We call it "Evolution". The Greeks called it *Phusis*, a word which we translate by "Nature", but which seems to mean more exactly "growth", or "the process of growth."[1] It is Phusis which gradually shapes or tries to shape every living thing into a more perfect form. It shapes the seed, by infinite and exact gradations, into the oak; the blind puppy into the good hunting dog; the savage tribe into the civilized city. If you analyse this process, you find that Phusis is shaping each thing towards the fulfilment of its own function—that is, towards the good. Of course Phusis sometimes

[1] See a paper by Professor J. L. Myres, "The Background of Greek Science", *University of California Chronicle*, xvi, 4.

fails; some of the blind puppies die; some of the seeds never take root. Again, when the proper development has been reached, it is generally followed by decay; that, too, seems like a failure in the work of Phusis. I will not consider these objections now; they would take us too far afield, and we shall need a word about them later. Let us in the meantime accept this conception of a force very like that which most of us assume when we speak of evolution; especially, perhaps, it is like what Bergson calls *La Vie* or *L'Élan Vital* at the back of *L'Évolution Creatrice*, though to the Greeks it seemed still more personal and vivid; a force which is present in all the live world, and is always making things grow towards the fulfilment of their utmost capacity. We see now what goodness is; it is living or acting according to Phusis, working with Phusis in her eternal effort towards perfection. You will notice, of course, that the phrase means a good deal more than we usually mean by living "according to nature". It does not mean "living simply", or "living like the natural man". It means living according to the spirit which makes the world grow and progress.

This Phusis becomes in Stoicism the centre of much speculation and much effort at imaginative understanding. It is at work everywhere. It is like a soul, or a life-force, running through all matter as the "soul" or life of a man runs through all his limbs. It is the soul of the world. Now, it so happened that in Zeno's time the natural sciences had made a great advance, especially astronomy, botany, and natural history. This fact had made people familiar with the notion of natural law. Law was a principle which ran through all the movements of what they called the *cosmos*, or "ordered world". Thus Phusis, the life of the world, is, from another point of view, the Law of Nature; it is the great chain of causation by which all events occur; for the Phusis which shapes things towards their end acts always by the laws of causation. Phusis is not a sort of arbitrary personal goddess, upsetting the natural order; Phusis is the natural order, and nothing happens without a cause.

A natural law, yet a natural law which is alive, which is itself life. It becomes indistinguishable from a purpose, the purpose of the great world-process. It is like a fore-seeing, fore-thinking power—*Pronoia*; our common word "Providence" is the Latin translation of this *Pronoia*, though of course its meaning has been rubbed down and cheapened in the process of the ages. As a principle of providence or forethought it comes to be regarded as God, the nearest approach to a definite personal God which is admitted by the austere logic of Stoicism. And, since it must be in some sense material, it is made of the finest material there is; it is made of fire, not ordinary fire, but what they called intellectual fire. A fire which is present in a warm, live man, and not in a cold, dead man; a fire which has consciousness and life, and is not subject to decay. This fire, Phusis, God, is in all creation.

We are led to a very definite and complete Pantheism. The Sceptic begins to make his usual objections. "God in worms?" he asks. "God in fleas and dung beetles?" And, as usual, the objector is made to feel sorry that he spoke. "Why not?" the Stoic answers; "cannot an earthworm serve God? Do you suppose that it is only a general who is a good soldier? Cannot the lowest private or camp attendant fight his best and give his life for his cause? Happy are you if you are serving God, and carrying out the great purpose as truly as such-and-such an earthworm." That is the conception. All the world is working together. It is all one living whole, with one soul through it. And, as a matter of fact, no single part of it can either rejoice or suffer without all the rest being affected. The man who does not see that the good of every living creature is his good, the hurt of every living creature his hurt, is one who wilfully makes himself a kind of outlaw or exile: he is blind, or a fool. So we are led up to the great doctrine of the later Stoics, the Συμπαθεία τῶν ὅλων, or Sympathy of the Whole; a grand conception, the truth of which is illustrated in the ethical world by the feelings of good men, and in the world of natural science. . . . We moderns may be excused for feeling a little surprise. . . . by the fact that the stars twinkle. It is because they are so sorry for us: as well they may be!

Thus Goodness is acting according to Phusis, in harmony with the will of God. But here comes an obvious objection. If God is all, how can anyone do otherwise? God is the omnipresent Law; God is all Nature; no one can help being in harmony with Him. The answer is that God is in all except in the doings of bad men. For man is free. . . . How do we know that? Why, by a *kataléptikê phantasia*, a comprehensive sense impression which it is impossible to resist. Why it should be so we cannot tell. "God might have preferred chained slaves for His fellow-workers; but, as a matter of fact, he preferred free men." Man's soul, being actually a portion of the divine fire, has the same freedom that God Himself has. He can act either with God or against Him, though, of course, when he acts against Him he will ultimately be overwhelmed. Thus Stoicism grapples with a difficulty which no religion has satisfactorily solved.

It will be observed that by now we have worked out two quite different types of Stoic—one who defies the world and one who works with the world; and, as in Christianity, both types are equally orthodox. We have first the scorner of all earthly things. Nothing but goodness is good; nothing but badness bad. Pain, pleasure, health, sickness, human friendship and affection, are all indifferent. The truly wise man possesses his soul in peace; he communes with God. He always, with all his force, wills the will of God; thus everything that befalls him is a fulfilment of his own will and good. A type closely akin to the early Christian ascetic or the Indian saint.

And in the second place we have the man who, while accepting the doctrine that only goodness is good, lays stress upon the definition of goodness. It is acting according to Phusis, in the spirit of that purpose or forethought which, though sometimes failing, is working always unrestingly for the good of the world, and which needs its fellow-workers. God is helping the whole world; you can only help a limited fraction of the world. But you can try to work in the same spirit. There were certain old Greek myths which told how Heracles and other heroes had passed laborious lives serving and helping humanity, and in the end became gods. The

Stoics used such myths as allegories. That was the way to heaven; that was how a man may at the end of his life "become not a dead body, but a star". In the magnificent phrase which Pliny translates from a Greek Stoic, God is that, and nothing but that; man's true God is the helping of man: *Deus est mortali iuvare mortalem.*

No wonder such a religion appealed to kings and statesmen and Roman governors. Nearly all the successors of Alexander—we may say all the principal kings in existence in the generations following Zeno—professed themselves Stoics. And the most famous of all Stoics, Marcus Aurelius, found his religion not only in meditation and religious exercises, but in working some sixteen hours a day for the good practical government of the Roman Empire.

Is there any real contradiction or inconsistency between the two types of Stoic virtue? On the surface certainly there seems to be; and the school felt it, and tried in a very interesting way to meet it. The difficulty is this: what is the good of working for the welfare of humanity if such welfare is really worthless? Suppose, by great labour and skill, you succeed in reducing the death-rate of a plague-stricken area; suppose you make a starving countryside prosperous; what is the good of it all if health and riches are in themselves worthless, and not a whit better than disease and poverty?

The answer is clear and uncompromising. A good bootmaker is one who makes good boots; a good shepherd is one who keeps his sheep well; and even though good boots are, in the Day-of-Judgement sense, entirely worthless, and fat sheep no whit better than starved sheep, yet the good bootmaker or good shepherd must do his work well or he will cease to be good. To be good he must perform his function; and in performing that function there are certain things that he must "prefer" to others, even though they are not really "good". He must prefer a healthy sheep or a well-made boot to their opposites. It is thus that Nature, or Phusis, herself works when she shapes the seed into the tree, or the blind puppy into the good hound. The perfection of the tree or hound is in itself indifferent, a thing of no ultimate value. Yet the goodness of Nature lies in working for that perfection.

Life becomes, as the Stoics more than once tell us, like a play which is acted or a game played with counters. Viewed from outside, the counters are valueless; but to those engaged in the game their importance is paramount. What really and ultimately matters is that the game shall be played as it should be played. God, the eternal dramatist, has cast you for some part in His drama, and hands you the role. It may turn out that you are cast for a triumphant king; it may be for a slave who dies in torture. What does that matter to the good actor? He can play either part; his only business is to accept the role given him, and to perform it well. Similarly, life is a game of counters. Your business is to play it in the right way. He who set the board may have given you many counters; He may have given you few. He may have arranged that, at a particular point in the game, most of your men shall be swept accidentally off the board. You will lose the game; but why should you mind that? It is your play that matters, not the score that you happen to make. He is not a fool to judge you by your mere success or failure. Success· or failure is a thing He can determine without stirring a hand. It hardly interests Him. What interests Him is the one thing which he cannot determine—the action of your free and conscious will.

This view is so sublime and so stirring that at times it almost deadens one's power of criticism. Let us see how it works in a particular case. Suppose your friend is in sorrow or pain, what are you to do? In the first place, you may sympathize—since sympathy runs all through the universe, and if the stars sympathize surely you yourself may. And of course you must help. That is part of your function. Yet, all the time, while you are helping and sympathizing, are you not bound to remember that your friend's pain or sorrow does not really matter at all? He is quite mistaken in imagining that it does. Similarly, if a village in your district is threatened by a band of robbers, you will rush off with soldiers to save it; you will make every effort, you will give your life if necessary. But suppose, after all, you arrive too late, and find the inhabitants with their throats cut and the village in ruins—why should you mind? You know it does not matter a straw whether the villagers' throats are cut or not cut; all that matters is how they behaved in the hour of death. Mr. Bevan, whose studies of the *Stoics and Sceptics* form a rare compound of delicate learning and historical imagination, says that the attitude of the Stoic in such a case is like that of a messenger boy sent to deliver a parcel to someone, with instructions to try various addresses in order to find him. The good messenger boy will go duly to all the addresses, but if the addressee is not to be found at any of them what does that matter to the messenger boy? He has done his duty, and the parcel itself has no interest for him. He may return and say he is sorry that the man cannot be found; but his sorrow is not heartfelt. It is only a polite pretence.

The comparison is a little hard on the Stoics. No doubt they are embarrassed at this point between the claims of high logic and of human feeling. But they meet the embarrassment bravely. "You will suffer in your friend's suffering", says Epictetus. "Of course you will suffer. I do not say that you must not even groan aloud. Yet in the centre of your being do not groan! Ἔσωθεν μέντοι μὴ στενάξῃς." It is very like the Christian doctrine of resignation. Man cannot but suffer for his fellow-man; yet a Christian is told to accept the will of God and believe that ultimately, in some way which he does not see, the Judge of the World has done right.

Finally, what is to be the end after this life of Stoic virtue? Many religions, after basing their whole theory of conduct on stern duty and self-sacrifice and contempt for pleasure, lapse into confessing the unreality of their professions by promising the faithful as a reward that they shall be uncommonly happy in the next world. It was not that they really disdained pleasure; it was only that they speculated for a higher rate of interest at a later date. Notably, Islam is open to that criticism, and so is a great deal of popular

Christianity. Stoicism is not. It maintains its ideal unchanged.

You remember that we touched, in passing, the problem of decay. Nature shapes things towards their perfection, but she also lets them fall away after reaching a certain altitude. She fails constantly, though she reaches higher and higher success. In the end, said the Stoic—and he said it not very confidently, as a suggestion rather than a dogma—in the very end, perfection should be reached, and then there will be no falling back. All the world will have been wrought up to the level of the divine soul. That soul is Fire; and into that Fire we shall all be drawn, our separate existence and the dross of our earthly nature burnt utterly away. Then there will be no more decay or growth; no pleasure, no disturbance. It may be a moment of agony, but what does agony matter? It will be ecstasy and triumph, the soul reaching its fiery union with God.

The doctrine, fine as it is, seems always to have been regarded as partly fanciful, and not accepted as an integral part of the Stoic creed. Indeed, many Stoics considered that if this Absorption in Fire should occur, it could not be final. For the essence of Goodness is to do something, to labour, to achieve some end; and if Goodness is to exist the world process must begin again. God, so to speak, cannot be good unless he is striving and helping. Phusis must be moving upward, or else it is not Phusis.

Thus Stoicism, whatever its weaknesses, fulfilled the two main demands that man makes upon his religion: it gave him armour when the world was predominantly evil, and it encouraged him forward when the world was predominantly good. It afforded guidance both for the saint and the public servant. And in developing this two-fold character I think it was not influenced by mere inconstancy. It was trying to meet the actual truth of the situation. For in most systems it seems to be recognized that in the Good Life there is both an element of outward striving and an element of inward peace. There are things which we must try to attain, yet it is not really the attainment that matters; it is the seeking. And, consequently, in some sense, the real victory is with him who fought best, not with the man who happened to win. For beyond all the accidents of war, beyond the noise of armies and groans of the dying, there is the presence of some eternal Friend. It is our relation to Him that matters.

A Friend behind phenomena: I owe the phrase to Mr. Bevan. It is the assumption which all religions make, and sooner or later all philosophies. The main criticism which I should be inclined to pass on Stoicism would lie here. Starting out with every intention of facing the problem of the world by hard thought and observation, resolutely excluding all appeal to tradition and mere mythology, it ends by making this tremendous assumption, that there is a beneficent purpose in the world and that the force which moves nature is akin to ourselves. If we once grant that postulate, the details of the system fall easily into place. There may be some overstatement about the worthlessness of pleasure and worldly goods; though, after all, if there is a single great purpose in the universe, and that purpose good, I think we must admit that, in comparison with it, the happiness of any individual at this moment dwindles into utter insignificance. The good, and not any pleasure or happiness, is what matters. If there is no such purpose, well, then the problem must all be stated afresh from the beginning.

A second criticism, which is passed by modern psychologists on the Stoic system, is more search-ing but not so dangerous. The language of Stoicism, as of all ancient philosophy, was based on a rather crude psychology. It was over-intellectualized. It paid too much attention to fully conscious and rational processes, and too little attention to the enormously larger part of human conduct which is below the level of consciousness. It saw life too much as a series of separate mental acts, and not sufficiently as a continuous, ever-changing stream. Yet a very little correction of statement is all that it needs. Stoicism does not really make reason into a motive force. It explains that an "impulse", or ὁρμή, of physical or biological origin rises in the mind prompting to some action, and then Reason gives or withholds its assent (συγκατάθεσις). There is nothing seriously wrong here.

Other criticisms, based on the unreality of the ideal Wise Man, who acts without desire and makes no errors, seem to me of smaller importance. They depend chiefly on certain idioms or habits of language, which, though not really exact, convey a fairly correct meaning to those accustomed to them.

But the assumption of the Eternal Purpose stands in a different category. However much refined away, it remains a vast assumption. We may discard what Professor William James used to call "Monarchical Deism" or our own claim to personal immortality. We may base ourselves on Evolution, whether of the Darwinian or the Bergsonian sort. But we do seem to find, not only in all religions, but in practically all philosophies, some belief that man is not quite alone in the universe, but is met in his endeavours towards the good by some external help or sympathy. We find it everywhere in the unsophisticated man. We find it in the unguarded self-revelations of the most severe and conscientious Atheists. Now, the Stoics, like many other schools of thought, drew an argument from this consensus of all mankind. It was not an absolute proof of the existence of the Gods or Providence, but it was a strong indication. The existence of a common instinctive belief in the mind of man gives at least a presumption that there must be a good cause for that belief.

This is a reasonable position. There must be some such cause. But it does not follow that the only valid cause is the truth of the content of the belief. I cannot help suspecting that this is precisely one of those points on which Stoicism, in company with almost all philosophy up to the present time, has gone astray through not sufficiently realizing its dependence on the human mind as a natural biological product. For it is very important in this matter to realize that the so-called belief is not really an intellectual judgement so much as a craving of the whole nature.

It is only of very late years that psychologists have begun to realize the enormous dominion of those forces in man of which he is normally unconscious. We cannot escape as easily as these brave men dreamed from the grip of the blind powers beneath the threshold. Indeed, as I see philosophy after philosophy falling into this unproven belief in the Friend behind phenomena, as I find that I myself cannot, except for a moment and by an effort, refrain from making the same assumption, it seems to me that perhaps here too we are under the spell of a very old ineradicable instinct. We are gregarious animals; our ancestors have been such for countless ages. We cannot help looking out on the world as gregarious animals do; we see it in terms of humanity and of fellowship. Students of animals under domestication have shown us how the habits of a gregarious creature, taken away from his kind, are shaped in a thousand details by reference to the lost pack which is no longer there—the pack which a dog tries to smell his way back to all the time he is out walking, the pack he barks to for help when danger threatens. It is a strange and touching thing, this eternal hunger of the gregarious animal for the herd of friends who are not there. And it may be, it may very possibly be, that, in the matter of this Friend behind phenomena, our own yearning and our own almost ineradicable instinctive conviction, since they are certainly not founded on either reason or observation, are in origin the groping of a lonely-souled gregarious animal to find its herd or its herd-leader in the great spaces between the stars.

At any rate, it is a belief very difficult to get rid of.

III

The Conception of Another Life

III

THE CONCEPTION OF ANOTHER LIFE

ALL we gregarious beings are swept along in the great stream of obvious social life. We are caught in the wheels of an enormous engine, pushed and carried by the half-conscious drift of the herd. And no doubt, as a rule, while things go entirely well with us, this is all the life we need. Yet constantly, in a man's ordinary experience, there is an undercurrent of discontent or homesickness; a feeling that this is not our complete or ultimate life; that there is somewhere another life which is more our own and which matters more. The commonest view places it after death, but mystics and contemplatives have believed it to exist now in our own souls. In any case it is described as something peculiarly real and transcendantly important. Indeed the language used about it, and about the rewards and punishments which it carries with it, is usually so strong as to excite suspicion in the plain man. The offer of such enormous interest seems calculated to compensate for some exceptionally large element of uncertainty.

The object of the present paper is to suggest some thoughts about the history of this widespread conception of Another Life, and then to make some comments on its validity.

This conception, it will be seen at once, is not the same as the immortality of the soul. Either might exist without the other. Suppose, in the words of the Fourth Book of Esdras, "*The Most High hath created not one world but two*", it does not necessarily follow that one of them lasts for ever. Man might be mortal and yet have an inner life more important than his outward life. And again one might have an immortality which was shadowy and unimportant.

For example, in what we may call the classic tradition of Greek poetry there are conceptions of immortality which for our present purpose can be disregarded. In Homer as a rule there is some life beyond the grave, but it is a feebler life. The psychology is of course confused. At one time the man's soul still lives in his other home, but the man himself is dead on the earth, torn by dogs and birds. At another time the man himself is in Hades, but he is only part of himself. There is breath; there is a phantom shape; but something is lacking which the primitive psychologist finds it hard to describe. There are no φρένες in him—literally no midriff; or again there is no life-blood. And the dead without life-blood are flitting shadows.

Even in a document like Aeschylus's *Choëphoroe*, where the whole plot turns on the awakening of the dead, it is a very dim awakening. Agamemnon lies motionless in his grave; he can just, after due ritual, be stirred to hear the cry of his children and to drink their drink-offerings. He is stung to life for a moment by the memory of a great anger, and then sinks back into the old sleep.

These Homeric conceptions, when analysed, have been shown to correspond to two separate strata of funeral customs, burning and burial. The shadowy ghost, the thing of air, is that θυμός or *Animus* which has passed away in the smoke of the funeral pyre; the more solid earth-folk, χθόνιοι, or ἔνεροι, to whom libations are poured through holes in the ground, are the dead lying in their graves. Both worlds, of course, are influenced by dreams and memories. The dead man is conceived as still performing his characteristic actions or bearing the death-wounds which we cannot forget. Hector appears *raptatus bigis ut quondam*.

Of course, this kind of life beyond the grave can be idealized. We find it set in an ancient garden beyond all seas, at the "springs of night and openings of Heaven"; in some region not shaken by wind or storm, far away, to be reached only by making the great leap over the Rock of Leucas and passing the ocean river to the Δῆμος Ὀνείρων, the old Land of Dreams.[1] But it is only a land of dreams; it is not a reality that reduces this present world to a dream. And it is that that we are looking for.

To find that kind of Other Life in Greek literature we must go to a different stream of tradition, a stream interrupted by gaps, known to us chiefly by allusions and not by positive statements, hard to trace to a definite authentic source, yet all the same clear and constant. In the Homeric Hymn to Demeter (l. 480) we hear of certain people who are for ever blessed, and others who are for ever deprived of their portion. If we ask who they are respectively, the answer is simple: the Initiated of Eleusis and the Uninitiated. The same conception occurs frequently in Pindar. In the Second Olympian, in practically all the θρῆνοι or Dirges—a natural place—we hear of the infinite consequences which a man's "holiness" or "unholiness" brings him in the Other Life. Indeed the body, in which our present life centres, is nothing permanent; it must die. There is something else which is greater, which lives on, which is indeed

[1] *Odyssey* vi. 43; iv. 563; Sophocles fr. 870; *Odyssey* xxiv. 11 ff.

the only part of man that comes really from God. It is by our ordinary standards a thing infinitely frail, αἰῶνος ἐίδωλον, "the reflection of a breath"; it sleeps while the limbs are in action, but when the noisy, restless body is once hushed it sees, or perhaps reveals, things beyond mortal sight. And hereafter, in the world beyond death, there is long peace and joy for the Blessed Heroes, for the Innocent, for those who "have endured even thrice"—let us observe the phrase—and kept their hands free from sin. And there are others suffering . . . what? Ah, Pindar is a writer of the high classic style; he will not soil his page with the description of torments. It is only "toil that eyes dare not look upon".

Again and again in Plato we find this same thought; in the *Phaedo*, in the *Phaedrus*, several times in the *Republic*. It is expounded at some length in Book X. It is parodied in Aristophanes's *Frogs*, parodied in detail after detail, with a freedom of allusion which indicates it as a doctrine widely familiar. It must clearly have been so, apart from the literary evidence, because it was exhibited to all Greece at Delphi, in the famous painting of Polygnotus, which portrayed the joys of Heaven and the pains of Hell almost in the style of the Campo Santo at Pisa. References to the same conception are scattered about freely in classical literature, in Euripides, in the Speech against Aristogeiton, in the fragments of Empedocles, in the gold tablets discovered in graves at Petelia and elsewhere,[1] in quite a number of funeral inscriptions. Most of the passages are collected in Professor Dieterich's book, *Nekyia*. It is needless to examine the evidence in detail, but there is a highly significant point to be observed: wherever we meet this particular conception of an immensely important future life, involving rewards and punishments, which in modern language we could describe as Heaven and Hell, it is in every case connected with Mysteries and Initiations. Sometimes it is the Eleusinian Mysteries; often the Orphic or Pythagorean; sometimes again the allusions are simply to Dionysus or Osiris or the Satyrs, or to other initiations such as were abundant in the Greek world.

He who believes and is initiated shall be saved; he who is not initiated shall be cast out. That is the normal rule of all exclusive religions, a rule which tends to seem natural and right to those inside and obviously preposterous to those outside. We hear of a famous jibe of Diogenes the Cynic at the idea that one Pataikion, an initiated burglar, should go to everlasting bliss

[1] These tablets are accessible in the Appendix to Miss Harrison's *Prolegomena to Greek Religion*, or in Guthrie's *Orpheus* (Cambridge 1935).

while the great Epaminondas is cast into torment.[1] Of course Diogenes is right; we all agree with him. But we should realize that to the pious Orphic it probably did not seem conceivable that a man could really be initiated, and receive his initiation properly, and hold firmly all the true doctrine and perform the blessed rites, and still be a bad man. He might perhaps err or slip, fall into sin, in extreme cases even into a burglary . . . but his heart must after all be in the right place. Orpheus or Osiris or the Mother can purify him of his accidental errors. In any case he is far preferable to those whited sepulchres who pass as good citizens, who commit no positive crimes perhaps, but have never had the inner filth cleansed from their souls, and never given their hearts to the true God. For all practical purposes the *Amuêtos* is *Anosios*, the Uninitiated is Unholy.

And what were the Mysteries? Thirty years ago, or even less, the question would have raised a sigh of weariness. It had too often been asked fruitlessly, and sensible men had simply set it aside. Any scholar who wrote about the Mysteries was supposed to need a truss of hay on his horns. And now the question is solved and the answer known. It came partly through Mannhardt and

[1] Plutarch, "de audiendis poetis", p. 21 E.

127

Frazer and Spencer and Gillen. It is specially made clear by the writings of Webster and Schurtz, whose results again are well criticized in Van Gennep's *Rites de Passage*. The Mysteries are simply Initiation Ceremonies, and initiation ceremonies are a normal feature of primitive society over the greater part of the globe. The age appointed for a boy's initiation varies, and sometimes there are many successive initiations; but as a normal type we may say that initiation is a ceremony emphasizing the vital moment when a boy, παῖς, becomes a man, ἀνήρ. The novice puts away childish things and takes upon him manly things. His ἀνδρεία—his manhood —is put to the ordeal; he is instructed in the full knowledge of his elders and ancestors; he is admitted to the three great duties of a full man of the tribe—to slay the tribe's enemies, to beget the tribe's children, and last but not least to speak with full knowledge in the tribal council.

In studying these tribal initiations in detail any imaginative student will be struck by two sides of them. There is a grotesque and ugly side, proper to the low level of culture from which they spring; and a sublime side, proper to the permanent spirit of man struggling to find its way. The initiations are in essence an emphasis, an over-emphasis, of something that in itself is true and fine. To the boy it is the dedication of himself to his life's work. He wants to be a man, a warrior, a counsellor. For that he is ready to bear ordeals of privation, pain, and terror, to face the most terrific arcana of his religion, ready even to die. For in the more complete initiations the novices are regularly supposed to be killed, to move for a time among the dead, to see gods and daemons and their own great ancestors, and afterwards, completely changed, with a new name, and a new personality, to be born again to this world.

We have seen that these conceptions of Another Life consisting of bliss and torments are, in ancient literature, always connected with the Mysteries. The writer wishes now to point out, or at least to suggest, that the mental pictures of Heaven and Hell which were current in ancient times and are still to a certain extent traditional among us, are based upon the actual ritual of the Mysteries. The scenery and arrangements, so to speak, of the other world are, in the first instance, projections of the initiation ceremonies.

The full mustering of the historical evidence on this point would need a large volume. But the point at issue can be illustrated by taking one good typical description of Heaven and Hell and showing how many of its details correspond with what we know of modern and ancient initiation rites. For instance, there is an early Christian document, which is also, as Dieterich has proved, quite in the pagan tradition, the so-called *Apocalypse of Peter*. It was found on a papyrus at Achmin and belongs to the second century. The following passages may be quoted:

"The Lord said: Let us go away to the Mountain."

This is normal in initiations. The initiands are taken away from human society, often to a mountain, sometimes to a forest. Compare the Cretan and Dionysiac Oreibasiai or Mountain-Rites.

"We begged him to show us one of our brethren, the righteous who have departed out of the world, that we might see what they are like in form and so bring comfort to men who hear us."

This is the normal aim or end of initiation ceremonies; cf. the accounts given in Schurtz, the Hermetic documents, and especially the account given by Appuleius, Book XI, of his own initiation.

"Two men appeared to whom we were not able to raise our eyes. Radiance came from their faces like the light of the sun, and their raiment was shining, such as the eye of man has never seen."

In the Eleusinia we have definite statements that the initiands were kept in darkness, and then dazzled and half-blinded by the appearance of divine beings in a blaze of light. A similar use of darkness followed by light is attested for savage mysteries. But let us note the next point.

"The bodies of these two beings were whiter than any snow and redder than any rose. I simply cannot express their beauty. Their hair was curly and bright coloured. It glowed over their faces and shoulders, like one crown woven of spikenard and flowers of all hues, or like a rainbow in the air."

Let us realize this description. Bodies snow-white and brilliant red, and hair all the colours of the rainbow standing out like a halo. A curiously exact counterpart to these blessed beings is to be found in the divine ministers, or πρόπολοι, who accompanied the God in initiations and represented the blessed ancestors. They were painted all over with white chalk and vermilion, while their hair was made to stick out in a halo, and was interwoven with ribbons and dyed grasses and brilliant objects of every colour. The evidence for the white and red is clear both for ancient and modern times. The hair is to be seen in any good collection of Papuan, Australian, or Polynesian photographs.

It is explained to Peter that these are the Righteous Departed; he asks where they live, and is shown

"a great place outside this world, shining with light, the soil of it blooming with immortal blossoms, and full of perfumes and sweet-smelling flowers. . . . The fragrance was so great that it was borne across even to this world."

This heaven seems like the region of light in which the divine beings appeared at the Eleusinia and in Appuleius's initiation. We may notice also the emphasis laid upon the sweet smells. Novices in initiations regularly pass through evil regions of darkness and foul smells and emerge into a heaven of light and fragrance. For the hierophant or stage-manager, if we may use such a word, the perfumes formed a comparatively easy and safe side of the revelation; easier certainly than the light and darkness.

And how were these blessed beings employed? The pseudo-Peter does not dwell on the point so long as some other Apocalyptists, but he speaks no less clearly. Just like the ministers of Dionysus or Isis or Mithras, or the Australian Durramulun, they were with one voice singing hymns to the glory of their god. The point, though so familiar, is instructive. This eternal hymn-singing has often been the subject of jokes: it strikes the outsider as odd and monotonous, but if we refer it to the ceremony from which it arose it is natural enough. Our savage stage-manager, who has to produce a brief and dazzling vision of the Blessed surrounding the Mystery of

God, naturally accompanies his blaze of light and perfume with a blaze of song. The awkwardness, if it is one, arises only when the song is made everlasting, when the outburst of one dazzling moment is transformed into a normal employment for the whole of life.

After this the pseudo-Peter passes to the description of hell. The first note struck is that of filth, the second darkness; then came tormenting angels in dark raiment. Especially prominent is the lake of mud, of mud and fire, of indescribable filth and blood and putrefaction, which recurs in slightly different forms again and again. The wicked are plunged in it, to varying depths, head first or otherwise.

The mire and filth of Hades are emphasized by Plato and Aristophanes and others, and the source of the conception is clear. Mud and filth were used in ancient initiation ordeals and purifications; and "immersion in dust and filth" is given by Webster as one of the commonest ordeals in savage initiation ceremonies. There is no need to prove this point in detail. But it is worth remembering that a pious savage's feeling about dirt is probably very different from ours. To us dirt is no doubt a highly disagreeable thing, but it is purely temporary and superficial, to be removed by a wash or a rinse. To the savage any dirt really worthy of the name is a thing of religious horror, polluting to the soul and unpurgeable. Mr. Edwyn Bevan has published an interesting story of the unspeakable horror produced in the mind of a pious Brahman by the English habit of using a toothbrush; to put every day into one's mouth—actually one's mouth!—the bone of a dog covered with the bristles of a pig . . . his imagination reeled at the wanton loathsomeness.

So much for the mire. It is naturally in a pit or depression of some kind. In many initiations the novices have to go down into a pit or chasm. In Crete and elsewhere they descended into a cave; in the rites of Trophonius into an artificial chasm, where they presently lost consciousness.

Some of Peter's sufferers were in a pit full of snakes. There were snakes in the pit of Trophonius, and snakes were largely used in the Bacchic rites. They naturally bit the wicked and caressed the initiated. The evidence on this point is abundant for ancient times, and we may compare the well-known snake dances of the Hopi and other Indians.

Other sufferers are scourged by daemons. Scourging is normal in ancient hells and ancient initiation ceremonies; we think of the celebrated ordeal at the altar of Artemis Orthia. The scourging of Australasian and African rites is apt to be performed by disguised daemons or spirits of the dead.

Others of Peter's victims scourge one another. One remembers the battles of youths which form a well-known ritual in ancient times, but it is not easy to find this particular variety of ordeal in an actual initiation ceremony. The present writer, however, has heard of a case where two Navajos, who wished to expiate their sins by scourging, found it more satisfactory to hit one another than for each to hit himself.

Others are tormented in various ways with fire and fire-brands. Ordeals of fire are, of course, common. In Australasian initiations great use is made of burning sticks to terrify or torment the novices. The Erinyes habitually carried fire-brands. Dionysus in one of his mystic epiphanies came as fire, and so did divers other gods. This fire, as we might expect, followed the example of the snakes: it burnt the wicked and spared the initiated, as Euripides has described in the *Bacchae*.

Other offenders are thrown over precipices, picked up at the bottom and thrown over again, and so on for ever. This form of torment is a little puzzling. To make a guilty man leap over a rock into the sea was a fairly common ritual in Greece for expiating a crime or purifying a community. Normally the leaper had his chance of swimming, and one does not hear of his being thrown over again. Precipitation was also a regular form of ritual execution; we think at once of the Barathron and the Tarpeian Rock, and especially of the Rock of Leucas, which became a mystical synonym for death. It is beyond that rock that Homer's world of the dead begins. And it may be that this form of torment was taken not from an initiation rite, but simply from a form of legal punishment. In initiations you could not, unless in very exceptional circumstances, afford to throw your novices over a real precipice. Yet a question arises in one's mind whether the tragic hoax played on Gloucester in *King Lear* has perhaps some ritual tradition behind it. Was it possibly an ordeal in some initiations to set the novice, blindfold or in the dark, on the top of some harmless little bank, tell him that he was on the edge of an awful precipice and order him to throw himself over? From all one reads of the dazed and half-insane condition in which the novices emerge from their ordeals, it would probably be easier to play this trick on them than it was on Gloucester.

The Apocalypse of Peter is fragmentary, and perhaps that is the reason why it lacks many of the regular characteristics of apocalyptic hells and heavens. There is no tremendous Voice such as we find in other apocalypses, in Bacchic initiations and all the mysteries, ancient and modern, in which a part is played by the bull-roarer.[1] There is no mention of that Cup of Cold Water which alleviates the anguish of parching souls in many Orphic and Osirian prayers, or that "light place with a fountain of water in the midst of it" which figures, for instance, in the book of Enoch (cap. xxii). Neither is there any torment by poison. Generally there are furies or similar beings holding cups of torment or of maddening philtres, or at least of Lethe. Such drugs are a regular feature of savage initiations. "They give them pellitory bark and several intoxicating plants", says Lawson of the Tuscarora Indians,[2] "which make them go raving mad as ever were any people in the world; and you may hear them make the most dismal and hellish cries and howlings that ever human creature expressed."

It is hardly necessary to press the detailed evidence further. A student who compares the ancient conceptions of Hell and Heaven, at any rate as expressed in all the Graeco-Christian tradition—the Jewish apocalypses are greatly influenced by other historical considerations—

[1] See *Themis*, by J. E. Harrison, pp. 61–66.

[2] *History of Carolina*, pp. 380–382, quoted by Webster, *Primitive Secret Societies* (New York, 1908), p. 33, cf. ibid., p. 57, on the drinking of *wysoccan* = $\lambda\dot\eta\theta\eta$.

can hardly fail to see that they are intimately modelled on the Initiation Ritual—the Ordeal, the Vision, and the Re-birth. That is to say, Heaven is not primarily modelled on the palace, nor Hell on the torture chamber. In later times this statement would need qualifications. As the early Christians were persecuted they naturally began to hate their persecutors, and sometimes reshaped their conceptions of the future so as to satisfy that hatred. Some hells did become, in all probability, mainly projections of the torture chamber, mere orgies of unsatisfied passion. There is much of this in the pseudo-Peter. There grew to be more passion in both the hells and the heavens, a passion of frantic hatred against the persecutor, a passion of pity and revenge for the oppressed innocent. But, apart from such disturbing elements, the normal conception of Another Life after death has in pagan and Christian tradition been modelled on the experience of the novice or devotee in the initiation ceremony.

Let us now think again of these initiations as they presented themselves to the mind of a believer. Let us forget the chalk and vermilion, the bull-roarers and the patent frauds, the cruelties and absurdities. Let us take for guidance the dozen or so expressions of enthusiastic faith and gratitude towards the Mysteries that have come down to us from Greek times, and the fairly abundant evidence from Australia and North America which shows that the same enthusiasm and devotion are still evoked in our own day. What does the novice feel? He is faced with the great moment of his life, the ordeal which is to decide whether or no he is to become that greatest of things, a Man. (We omit for simplicity's sake all reference to female initiations, which were on the whole less prominent.) There is almost no bait of pleasure held out to the boy. Nothing but service and duty and self-respect. Everything that he has learned to admire is summed up in the achievement of manhood. A man must have perfect courage, true knowledge, and—in the sense in which he understands it—complete purity. All our modern witnesses express amazement at the endurance with which the Red Indian boys, without uttering a cry or moving a muscle, submit to be flogged almost to death, burned, mutilated, swung on hooks till the flesh breaks, and the like. And not only Red Indians, who are always brave, but Polynesians and Negroes and Australians. These physical ordeals are enough to stagger us; but one must suspect that ordeals of hunger and thirst, of the madness produced by strange drugs, of the ineffable terrors of the supernatural which they are compelled to face, are probably even a greater strain on the young men's constancy.

And we can see the meaning of it. It too is over-emphasis. The important thing in life for each of these boys is to become a man and all that a man should be. Now, as a matter of fact, becoming a man is a gradual process; in the full sense of the words it is a process which is being achieved, or not achieved, during the whole of life. This length, slowness, uncertainty, is just what puzzles and exasperates the natural human being in us. We want to get it over. "Give it us now," we cry: "pile on all the ordeals, all the terrors and temptations, in one mass and let us face them now, now: let us either be men once for all, or else be consumed with fire or left rotting in the pit." The experience of initiation thus acquires an enormous, a practically eternal significance.

In another way also this significance is deepened. All initiation ceremonies seem, if they last on, to pass through two stages. First, they are universally practised through the whole of a homogeneous tribe; next, after migrations, invasions, mixtures of races, and the like, they become the mark and property of a special society, a Church, as it were—usually more or less secret.

Initiations are only for the faithful; the higher

initiation is only for those who have passed through the lower. We hear of three grades: we hear of seven. Now, let us think of an early Christian, or, better perhaps, of a faithful adherent of any of the ancient Mystery Religions. They all lived in a wrecked or hostile world. "Zion hath been taken from us: we have nothing now save the Mighty One and His Law." The Jews themselves were rather averse from mysteries; but these words of Baruch express the feeling of many ruined and bewildered nations.[1] Greek or Egyptian or Syrian or Anatolian, the mystery devotee was living in a great callous world of foreign soldiers and traders and governors and *publicani*, a world in which he seemed to be born an exile and hardly understood the language in which he was plundered or governed. Would he not feel that his true life, the life that mattered and enabled him to feel that he truly lived, was that which he passed among his fellow-believers? Out in the market-place he could not speak of the things for which he cared most. Neighbours might be civil or uncivil, magistrates and soldiers honest or dishonest; they could only touch the outside of him. At night, in his own θίασος, he could meet those who felt with him and had the same needs as he. He spoke their

[1] Apocalypse of Baruch 85, 3: quoted by Burkitt, *Jewish and Christian Apocalypses* (1914).

language. He was rapt with them into the same ecstasies. He could read in their eyes a history like his own. They had laboured under the same burden of sin, had conceived the same hope, and attained the same deliverance. Here and there, doubtless, would be one who had achieved the human soul's ultimate adventure and been for some single infinite instant united to the living God. This, it is easy to see, would be to such a man the true life; and this is the life that would be projected by his imagination into eternity: an eternity in which every experience would be intensified; an eternity in which these tyrannous outsiders, these Roman magistrates and hard men of the world and committers of impurity, would be put to the ordeals and fail. How they would fail! Miserably, inevitably; from their bestial ignorance, their manifold defilements, their lack of any true Helper and Saviour, as well as their obvious deficiency in all finer qualities. Doubtless they would get through in time: after a thousand years, perhaps, or ten thousand or thirty thousand . . . at least all except the really bad ones. Hell proper is generally reserved, as Peter's Apocalypse vividly shows us, for those who have committed sins against the Church itself —apostates, betrayers, persecutors, and hostile witnesses.

Thus the initiated have a true life of their own

in this world, which is further strengthened by being projected into an imagined eternity.

Suppose now a man of more critical temper, a Jew, for instance, who is content to wrap himself in the Law, or—more instructive for our purpose—a Greek philosopher: one who does not believe the fables of the underworld nor yet the half-mad doctrines of the mystery-mongers. He does not yield himself up to "projections". He is severely anxious to keep to the seen and proven fact. Yet he will not go without his Other Life. Where is he to find it?

Stoic and Epicurean, the two poles of Greek philosophy, agree. The true life of man, the life that matters, is within. It is the life of the soul. The outer worldly life is real enough—the philosopher does not pretend that it is a mere dream or Maya—but it is of no consequence. The Stoic doctrine, as explained elsewhere in this book, is quite clear on this point. Life is like a play acted or a game played with counters. The play is only make-believe. The counters have no value: it matters not who wins or loses. All that matters is that the play should be acted well, the game played as it should be played. God is the judge and does not go by outward results. What interests Him is the one thing which He cannot determine, the action of your free will.

It is quite simple. Act one way and you are a

good thing; another, and you are a bad thing; and to be good or bad is heaven or hell. In this region of the free will lies the life that is your own, your true heaven, quite other than the obvious life, independent of it, untouched by it. For even Epicurus himself has confessed that the Good Man will be happy on the rack. Even the average unregenerate man confesses it in his heart. Give him the choice in his calm moments, while his nerves are still firm, to be either the martyr or the tyrant who tortures him; he will choose the martyr.

Fascinating, triumphant, almost irresistible, this great Stoic gospel seems at first sight to have rejected all mythology, all bribes and threats and dreams, and to have opened up a vision of the meaning of life as true as it is noble. But it is not so. This imaginary blessedness of the Wise Man, blessedness impervious to the shocks of fortune, to the pain of oneself or others, to the praise or blame, the love or hate, of all one's associates and fellow-creatures, is almost as deep a dream, almost as violent an over-emphasis, as the Elysium or Tartarus of the vulgar. The Stoics could see that the furies with their burning torches were only metaphors to denote a tormented mind. They tried hard to face the facts of life, to invent no fancied eternal recompense for the good or punishment for the evil, but to leave virtue strictly its own reward. They made the attempt with wonderful self-restraint, but the effort was too great for them. They cared so intensely about the matters at issue that they could not help over-emphasizing what they considered most important. And the passion of their over-emphasis almost created for itself a new mythology.

But apart from that, apart from the mere element of exaggeration in the Stoic conception of this inward untroubled life which belongs for ever to the righteous and the innocent, we may raise the question whether it was in its main direction a good ideal. Is it a good thing that we should accustom ourselves to feel, when we are cast down or disgusted by ordinary realities, that there is in our possession Another Life, more or less independent of the great stream, which matters infinitely more?

A strong case can be made against it, especially in these days when social duties are so much more valued than private virtues. Man is born a member of some society; his whole being is a network of intimate relations, of attractions and repulsions, helpings and hinderings, from which it is neither possible nor desirable that he should cut himself free. His relations to his fellow-men form, in normal circumstances, far the greater part of his happiness or unhappiness, even of his self-respect or his despair. For the most personal of all things, a man's own conscience, is mostly formed for him by other people. Anyone who tries first fully to realize the biological fact that man is a gregarious animal, and then, by an effort of introspection, to realize the infinitely complex stream of aims and impulses and affections on which he moves, must, it would seem, answer the Stoic claim with a definite rejection: Here or nowhere is man's true life; not in any imagined heaven, not in the rituals or dreams of any exclusive society; not even in the supposed calm of that treacherous fortress, a man's own soul.

And yet, on the other side, the voices of nearly all the saints and sages call to us in warning that this present obvious life cannot be all in all. For one thing the judgements of the herd are almost always wrong in value. If they do not often call bad things directly good and good bad, they constantly think cheap things precious and fine things unimportant. Everyone who cares at all for truth needs some court of appeal from the mere judgement of the world. The appeal will take various shapes and directions; but in the last analysis, when stripped of all its disguises, it will generally be an appeal exactly like that of the Stoics or of the seventeenth-century Quakers, from the world to one-self, from the now and here outwardly prevailing judgement to the judgement of one's inmost mind. One need not say that it is only that, much less that it is consciously that. In practice, for one thing, a man is hardly ever quite alone. He has his friends, his fellow-workers, his Church. They, in so far as they really support him, help to build up that Other Life whose canons are greater than the canons of the world. And, even when a man is quite alone, he generally feels himself to be appealing to some unknown friend, to the judgement of posterity, or to a righteous God. He projects another society to counterbalance the society which he has rejected; for a gregarious animal cannot be alone in heaven. But always he himself is the centre and pivot of this higher society of his own creating. It never really gives its verdict against him. If it did, it would have gone over to the enemy and would cease to be heaven. Its function is to fortify the man's own soul and enable him to defy his environment. The Stoic was so far right. There is another tribunal; and it is, ultimately, the tribunal of a man's own soul.

And not only a tribunal but also a refuge. The Stoic saw that too. Man must retire to that same inner region when he is strained and buffeted by the outer life, and needs peace or strengthening. For experience seems to show that those who have loved their kind most effectively have needed some refuge in which to be free from them. In order to help men you must be able to defy them. In order to give them the best you can, you must needs have within you something better, or at least more intimate, which you cannot give them. For how can you help and understand a man unless you are a separate and different person from him, standing on your own feet? And this is true not only of the selected Wise Man, described by Plato in words which at every turn are borrowed from the Mysteries, who deliberately descends into the cave to help his weaker brethren. It is true, in some degree, of every human being. We are, after all, individuals as well as members of a community. We are all, when a certain limit is passed, strangers one to another. There is a region in each of us where no other can penetrate; and every man is alone in his highest thoughts as every man is alone when he dies.

We are accustomed to treat this fact as something hard or piteous, a kind of horror in the background of life. Yet perhaps such a judgement is wrong. It is not a horror. It is only a necessary condition of social living, that we are individuals as well as members of a social whole. And it seems to be this nucleus of fact which lies at the root of most of the wide-spreading dreams that we have been dealing with. It is this truth, that the whole of our life cannot be contained by any human society but some part of the soul must be always alone—this truth so austere, so frail, a thing which we can so easily forget and which must never be forgotten—that has caused so much passionate dreaming and equally passionate denial. It has been over-emphasized in divers ways in different ages of history; set up as an ideal in contemplative societies; more enthusiastically glorified and concentrated in world-wide mysteries and initiations; projected beyond the bounds of the physical world in dreams of some ultimate perfect acceptance or utter rejection, some everlasting home or eternal exile. The truth itself, if properly understood, ought of course to be sufficient motive for good action; but man is slow, and likes his motives for good over-emphasized and made tremendous before he will stir.

There is, then, another tribunal to which we can appeal from the world's judgement; there is another life in which we can find some refuge. And doubtless, if we must have one of the tribunals against us, it is better that it should be the loud and violent outside tribunal with all its harsh sanctions, not the intimate and silent one which exercises no sanctions but permits of no escape. But the advocates of this Other Life must not promise too much. They must not speak to us of regions of light and truth made perfect, nor of fields unshaken by snow and tempest where joy grows like a tree. Our tribunal is not perfect; it only tries to see and to do right. Our refuge promises no eternal bliss. It gives only a rallying-point, a spell of peace in which to breathe and to think, a sense not exactly of happiness, but of that patience and courage which form at least a good working substitute for happiness. For real full-blooded happiness, as for any satisfaction of our complete natures, we are thrown for good and evil on the realities of the outer social life and the turbid mercies of our fellow-men.

IV

What is Permanent in Positivism

IV

WHAT IS PERMANENT IN POSITIVISM

AUGUSTE COMTE was actually born in the eighteenth century, and there is a touch of the eighteenth century in his thinking. By the time of his death in 1857 his influence was immense upon all progressive European thought. Nowadays he is awarded a very small place in most histories of philosophy, and the Church or organized body of teachers which he founded, once so brilliant and influential, may almost be described as moribund. Such neglect seems a sign of complete failure; but in reality it is due almost as much to the general acceptance of his main doctrines as to their rejection. No doubt he was overbold. He attempted to build a complete and final system of philosophy based upon all the sciences. Necessarily any such system was conditioned by the state of science at the time, by the social environment of post-Revolutionary France in which he lived, by the traditions of Catholicism by which he was surrounded. As the conditions have changed the system has ceased to fit. Also, the era of hope and confidence into which he was born, and which made the creation of his system possible, was succeeded by an age of mistrust in which scientists were shy of all wide principles and generalizations, and took refuge in their separate specialisms. The specialists had been his chief enemies in his lifetime and they triumphed over him after his death. Again, the two opposing armies of Faith and Science, whom he sought to reconcile, and who seemed in many ways to be approaching one another in the nineteenth century, seem now to have lost any particular desire to be reconciled. The Catholic Church holds as firmly as ever that it possesses the monopoly of truth, subject to no progressive reinterpretation. "That meaning of the sacred dogmas is to be perpetually retained which our Holy Mother, the Church, has once declared."[1] And the post-war sceptic on his side has no particular desire to reinterpret dogmas which have ceased to interest him.

Yet Comte was a very great figure in the history of thought, and Positivism remains a great coherent statement, imperfect indeed and showing signs of its period, of certain permanent and all-important truths.

One reason why Comte seems so often to have been superseded is that he often anticipated later

[1] Judgement on Dr. Mivart: Bridges, *Illustrations of Positivism*, 1907, p. 126.

thought or knowledge. Pioneers are always super-seded. Otherwise they would not be pioneers. His three stages—Theological, Metaphysical, Positive—differently phrased and subdivided, have become a commonplace of history and anthropology. His *nisus conativus*, taken presumably from Leibnitz, has become Bergson's *élan vital*. The word and the idea of "sociology" as a science, a conception destined to bear such abundant and ever-increasing fruit, were his invention.[1] He proved from the biological researches of Gall and others that unselfishness was not a miracle produced by divine grace in the selfish animal man; on the contrary, there were in man's nature not merely egoistic instincts concerned with self-preservation or the good of the *Ego*, but also social instincts concerned with the good or preservation of others, of "*autrui*"; and to describe them he invented the important word "altruism". It was he, following no doubt in the tracks of Montesquieu and others, who emphasized the growth of one civilization out of another, using the word "filiation", which in the form "affiliation" plays so large a part in, for instance, Mr. Toynbee's *Study of History*. It was perhaps a touch of prophetic foresight that made him long for that Society of Civilized Nations

[1] In 1837. The word was adopted by J. S. Mill and Spencer, who had both been groping towards the idea.

which he called "The Republic of the West", and expect a great renaissance in China with effects reverberating through the world. Among other views of his which roused the opposition of J. S. Mill and other generally sympathetic contemporaries but would find more support now among thinkers who are called progressive, were his insistence on the difference rather than the equality of Man and Woman; on the abundant faults and weaknesses of Democracy; and on Man's need for a Church and a system of prayer and worship, though not for a personal God.

This after all was his main problem. I will try to formulate it in the way that seems to me most intelligible.

Man is surrounded by unknown forces of infinite extent and almost infinite power. It is man's consciousness of these forces, or, shall we say, of the infinite extent of the Unknown compared with the small sphere of Knowledge in which we live, that constitutes the attitude towards life which we call a religious attitude. A man who never thinks at all about the Unknown but is confident that outside his approved range of knowledge there is nothing, or at least nothing that matters, is clearly without Religion; I conclude therefore that he is equally without religion whether his approved range is the *Encyclopaedia*

Britannica or the dogmas of some infallible Church. To be cock-sure is to be without religion. The essence of religion is the consciousness of a vast unknown. Call it Faith or call it Doubt: they are two sides of the same medal.

The most obvious reaction towards this vast unknown is Fear. *Primus in orbe deos fecit timor.* The more man is exposed to the action of the unknown the greater is his fear of it. Primitive man is helpless and therefore superstitious. Society, as it becomes civilized, is always protecting itself. Civilization consists largely in a process of building or extending the walls round that little island of space, that City or Fatherland, in which life is known and friendly, in order to keep off the infinite unfriendly and unknown that is outside. Hence the rigidity of custom, the fixed pattern of life, usual in primitive societies, and due to the omnipresent fear of that which is unknown, unaccustomed, unintelligible. Hence the superstition that grows in times of danger and dies down when life seems safe and the world kind.

How does man represent these forces to himself? Naturally, inevitably, his thinking is conditioned by his human nature. It is anthropomorphic in the fullest sense, including that for which Mill coined the awkward word "anthro-

157

pophuism." It sees everything in human terms. The old saying of Xenophanes, that if cattle or lions could picture the gods they would make them like cattle or lions, is more than superficially true. If man sometimes makes his gods in non-human form, in animal form like the Egyptians, in pillar or tree form like the Minoans, that does not alter the main fact of anthropomorphism; for the worshipper thinks of the animal or the pillar as having the same feelings as himself. He fears its anger; he appeases it with gifts, he cajoles it with compliments, avoids stirring its jealousy, and the like.

There is no essential difference here between what Comte calls "fetichism" and Dr. Marett "animatism" on the one hand, and ordinary polytheism on the other. Either the non-human object feared behaves like a man, or, if for some reason that conception strikes the worshippers as improbable, there is a more definitely anthropoid being connected with the object. If the torrent or the thunderbolt is not actually alive and angry, then an angry being in the background has swollen the torrent or thrown the thunderbolt. Man thinks in this way because he cannot help it. His gods see, hear, smell, touch, with human senses; are pleased and displeased, kind and hostile, just as men are. They are, though superhuman, human in nature. Mostly they are thought of as Fathers or members of the tribe and therefore on the whole as friends, but subject unfortunately to the most unpredictable impulses.

Man thinks anthropomorphically because he cannot help it. For the rest, most of his thinking is determined, in the general absence of other evidence, by his wishes and fears. The proportion between them depends, it would seem, mainly on the degree of security a particular society has attained. When insecure, a man is haunted by fears, and thinks of his gods as constantly needing propitiation. Sailors are traditionally superstitious, but have become much less so since the invention of large steamers has made them less dependent on the unknown. So are soldiers in wartime; so are refugees and the like. As life becomes safe, fears dwindle and wishes predominate. We wish never to die; we wish to have for ourselves and our own community, who are of course our friends and good, a life of eternal happiness; so we create Heaven. The bad, the uninitiated especially, those who have persecuted and wronged our friends and us, must be repaid in their own coin. For them there is Hell—a conception dependent originally on membership or non-membership of a sacred society, but kept alive by the wish for vengeance. A persecuted generation revels in the thought of the torments in store for its persecutors, as one sees from the various Apocalypses.[1]

That is the crude raw material of most religious belief. It soon passes into something more disinterested, more in accord with the higher development of human society. Man longs for something like Heaven and Hell to correct the intolerable injustices of this mortal world. Dante must have meant something when he spoke of Hell as created by

La somma sapienza e il primo amore.

Horrid as the paradox is, one can understand that man's natural sense of justice, maddened by the oppressions of the innocent, craves not merely that the innocent should be comforted but also that the oppressor should suffer. If we set aside the traditional though immoral claim of various organized Churches that Hell is the correct punishment for non-membership of their body, one can see that, apart from the direct desire for revenge on the persecutor, that passionate and disinterested sense of justice which lies near the foundation of society tends to create some "bright reversion in the sky" for the wrongs of mankind. I suspect it is this craving, carried to higher and subtler forms, which finds

[1] See p. 129, ff.

vent in books like the *Imitatio Christi* and the mystic dogmas or speculations of various creeds.

Here again, as in all the realm of wish-thinking, the lower and more selfish forms of wish tend to creep in, like weeds, into the garden of the ideal. We long for some higher law to set right the wrongs of the world. Yet, after all, do we really want all our own offences to be punished as they deserve? As Dr. Freud has pointed out, our attitude towards the Law, civil or moral, is always "ambivalent". We love it and uphold it as maintaining the wish or conscience of Society against wicked law-breakers who may do wrong to us and our community; but we feel, in our own exceptional case, a conscious or subconscious desire sometimes to escape from it. The gods, being human, can be got at, propitiated, persuaded. From the earliest times to the latest, special societies like the Orphics, the Brahmins, the Catholic Church, provide guaranteed processes of initiation, baptism, purification, absolution, by which to evade the due penalty for our offences.

A third characteristic of religious thought is its emotional quality, due, apparently, to a subconscious recognition that its most cherished doctrines are really mere wish-beliefs, not facts proved or provable, but hopes without which we cannot be happy. The craving for certainty where all is uncertain betrays itself by passionate and continual over-emphasis. Genuine intellectual certainty is generally serene; it does not seek to kill or burn those who differ from it in opinion.

It is not necessary to follow in any detail the course of criticism to which these anthropomorphic conceptions have been continually subjected from the time of Xenophanes onward. His splendid rejection of anthropomorphism as regards the outward form of the gods, or, as he preferred to say, of God, affected most Greek philosophic thought afterwards; but it is worth noting that, in spite of all his efforts, his dehumanized spherical God, though it has no eyes or ears or brain, but "sees, hears, and thinks with its whole being", nevertheless does "see, hear, and think"—which are, after all, human activities. So difficult is it to dehumanize our thought. Cicero ridicules the belief in *barbatum Iovem, galeatam Minervam* (*Nat. De.* 36). He recognizes that the visions in which various people have seen Jupiter with a beard or Minerva with a helmet are purely subjective, and have shown the divine being in the shape laid down by the social tradition. It was only a step further to see that the same social tradition was responsible not merely for the beard and the helmet, but for Jupiter and Minerva themselves. Being surrounded by unknown forces and seeking some-how to be on terms with them, Man made God in his own image. Throughout the whole process two influences are co-operating, which we may call man-thinking and wish-thinking. Man cannot help—at least not without extraordinary mental effort—thinking in human terms. The unknown forces which help and hinder him can only be thought of as moved by the motives and using the methods and instruments that he knows. And secondly, the thing that in his loneliness he wishes most is that some great Man, like himself but infinitely stronger, speaking his language and sharing his feelings of right and wrong, his friend-ships and his hatreds, should guide and protect his enterprises. The fishermen of the Greek islands liked to think of a Great Fisherman armed like themselves with a trident or fish-spear, presiding over their boats: so they created Poseidon. But, even if they could get free from their wishes, they could scarcely have conceived of their God in any other form. The form was dictated by the social tradition.

A very simple but attractive application of this principle was made by Freud in his book, *The Future of an Illusion*. The chief god of polytheists, the sole god of monotheists, is habitually called "Father", a plain projection of the human father or patriarch. The father in a simple patriarchal society has two main functions; abroad he is the protector of his family against enemies, at home he is the judge and punisher of the disobedient. He is thus both loved and feared. This relation is not merely primitive, it is pre-human. When a herd of gregarious animals, such as deer or cattle, is threatened by danger, they form up to meet it, the leader or patriarch in the front centre, the young bulls beside him, the cows behind, and the young calves well covered in the middle of the ring. There the patriarch is the protector; a very present help in trouble. But he is also a terror to the rebellious or disobedient if any younger bull disputes his rule.

The chief God is a Father, but he is also a King. And in Europe, since our religious literature comes almost entirely from Oriental sources, he is a King of the despotic Oriental type. The conception of God in the Old Testament shows several strands of influence. Like an earthly pastoral king he has tribute paid to him which is a pastoral tribute, the "first-born of every flock"; and, as on earth, the first-born can be redeemed. Like the Assyrian and Babylonian Kings in the British Museum he requires praise, continual praise, praise in all its forms; and, if the praise ever strikes him as insufficient, there is trouble for those responsible. He is jealous in the extreme, and likes constantly to dwell upon the

fact: "I the Lord, thy God, am a jealous God"
grows into "Jehovah whose name is Jealous"
(Exod. xxxiv. 14), the "name" standing for the
essential nature. His jealousy is directed against
other similar potentates, the gods of other
nations in the neighbourhood. They are all his
enemies, and woe betide anyone who speaks well
of them. His people are to "destroy their altars,
break their images, cut down their groves" (ibid.,
13). Any respect paid to them will be punished
by utter destruction (Deut. iv. 26); Jehovah's
jealousy will not be appeased until the third and
fourth generation (Deut. v. 9). The land of such
an offender will be sown with salt and brimstone
(Deut. xxix. 23), so that it shall never bear fruit
again—just as enemy land was treated by the
Mesopotamian tyrants in their worst anger. And
observe, though certain moral and legal offences
are properly condemned in the Laws, the sin
which above all others rouses Jehovah is Dis-
obedience to him, or attention to other gods.
For that, and for almost nothing else, he "smites":
indeed, the variety and ferocity of his smiting,
as detailed in Cruden's *Concordance*, would do
credit to the most ferocious of Oriental despots.[1]

[1] He smites the knees, the legs, the loins; he smites the
"land of Egypt", smites "all the first-born", smites "every
living thing"; he smites with frogs, pestilence, consump-
tion, fever, botch, scab, blindness, madness, great plague,
and a general curse.

On the other hand, his mercy or bounty is on the same great scale as that of Haroun al-Raschid or Suleiman the Magnificent; though apparently any absence of punishment counts as mercy because, being above the Law and having every right to smite his subjects as he pleases, he may well claim that it is kind of him not to smite them. I take these passages not for the purpose of ridiculing the magnificent records of ancient Israel, but to show how the Hebrews conceived of the unknown forces of the world as controlled by an anthropomorphic being, and how, further, they pictured that being partly in the guise of a pastoral patriarch and partly as a king of Babylon —only more formidable. The late Professor Kennett, one might add, has shown in a most interesting way how Jehovah has been affected by the sojourn of Israel in the desert. He has no consort; he is not concerned with fertility or interested in agriculture, but makes up for the vices which he is thereby spared by his arid and torrid severity. His extreme jealousy of the Baalim is explained by the fact that his chosen people when they came out of the desert and settled down to agricultural life were inevitably much tempted to practise the normal agricultural ceremonies. It would be curious to study the influence which this idea of the pastoral patriarch *plus* the Oriental despot still exercises over the imagination of Protestant Christendom.

It is perhaps this conception of God as an Oriental tyrant which gives rise in so many religions to the need of some kinder and more human being to mediate and intercede. In earthly despotisms it is usual, it is almost a necessity, that those who wish to make a request of the King should first make favour with some powerful subordinate who has access to him. It was a risky business to do so in person. When Pythios the Lydian, relying on promises of royal favour, asked Xerxes that his eldest son, instead of marching on Greece, might be left behind in Asia to comfort him, Xerxes granted the request by cutting the said son into two halves and leaving them. The mediator required is sometimes a woman, like Esther with Darius or Mme. de Maintenon with Louis XIV; sometimes a being like the Faithful Son of Babylonian religious art. Christianity in its Catholic form looks chiefly to the Virgin, in its Evangelical form to Jesus, as the eternal mediator between us common men and the "just wrath" of this formidable potentate.

One of the most striking differences between mediaeval and modern Christianity can be explained in the same way. God is the eternal judge. A mediaeval law court relied greatly on torture. Apart from man's natural enjoyment of cruelty, mediaeval society tried to make up for the inefficiency of its police system by extreme ferocity against those offenders whom it was able to catch. To strike terror was the duty and privilege of the earthly judge. The eternal judge must do the same and do it even better. He must apply eternal tortures, and of a kind far surpassing the puny efforts of earthly racks or flames. The modern world, on the other hand, has abolished torture, and regards the infliction of it by law as an abomination. Consequently, in spite of very explicit texts and an immense weight of uncontested tradition, modern civilized societies have either abolished Hell altogether or reformed it into something so metaphorical that it does not horrify the average conscience. I am disposed to think that one important element in this change of social psychology was the discovery of anaesthetics. Violent pain used, till lately, to be a normal element in human life: a thing to be shrieked over by the victim, commiserated or laughed at according to circumstances by the spectators, but never a strange unnecessary horror which ought to be entirely removed. Certainly some vast social change seems necessary to explain the distance we have moved from the state of mind indicated by certain well-known and hideous phrases in Dante, Thomas Aquinas, and even Augustine.

It will be observed that in all this list, which could be extended indefinitely, of changes in the conceptions man has formed of the God or gods of his worship, he never really gets away from either his man-thinking or his wish-thinking. In our own day it seems to me that both are being re-emphasized. The ordinary Christian apologist has almost forgotten to argue that his creed is true; he concentrates so exclusively on arguing that it is a comfort, a source of good life, a psychological necessity: in fact that the only way to be happy is to believe it, or perhaps not so much to believe it, but to accept and act upon it. That is confessedly wish-thinking. And at the same time there is a revival of extreme man-thinking in reaction against the impersonal theisms of philosophers like Green and Bradley, Kant and Spinoza. Emphasis is laid, not merely in evangelical circles but much more widely, on the worship of the man-god Jesus and the intimate personal relation which his wor-shippers claim to have established with him as with a human friend.

Is it possible to rid ourselves of these two weaknesses, man-thinking and wish-thinking, and yet retain any effective conception of God? I doubt it. A certain Arab mystic has made the trenchant criticism that to call God "righteous" implies just as profound anthropomorphism as to say that he has a beard. "He is just", "He is merciful", "He is long-suffering", "he loves mankind" . . . all such phrases apply to God human qualities and human ways of behaviour. Take them away, and you are left with some purely abstract residuum, indescribable and inconceivable: not even a Reason or an Intelligence or a Purpose, for each of these is essentially a human thing, an attribute of a limited being who has to think, plan and take pains. I see no escape from the conclusion that if you take away the humanity of God, you take away the traditional conception of God altogether. Theism in its essence, if it means anything, means that behind the dead inhuman world which cares nothing for us, there exists something human which does care; there is Fatherly Love, Providence, Foresight, or some other emphatically human quality: there is, in the phrase used in a previous essay, "A Friend behind phenomena."

Of course that is not all that is demanded by theism, at any rate in its higher forms. The friend must be something far better than any human friend, more loving, more powerful. I am not sure that the normal man, if left to himself, would insist that his god should be by human standards a thing of absolute perfection, either in goodness or in power. The Greek and Indian and Nordic gods were neither. Furthermore, a perfect being could hardly, I think, be, strictly speaking, the object of love. We love the suffering God, the human God. We love the Being who strives, who shows courage, who endures, hopes, and makes sacrifices; but a Being perfect in power can do none of these things. He can never make that appeal for sympathy which seems essential to the power of arousing love.[1] But two influences at least seem to have been at work demanding infinite perfection of God. Many philosophers, from Plato onwards, have insisted that any imperfection whatsoever is inconsistent with the divine nature; and those nations whose religious ideas were largely formed by the Old Testament, with its sublimated despot insisting on unlimited glorification, were forced to regard their own hymns of praise as true, and to believe that the Ruler of the world was endowed with all the virtues they ascribed to him, perfect justice, perfect wisdom, and perfect

---

[1] It is interesting to note that Aristotle in seeking τὸ πρῶτον κινοῦν, the First Cause which moves the rest of the universe but is not moved itself, decides that it does so as "an object of desire, or an object of thought", which equally is unmoved but causes movement (action) in others, and finally says κινεῖ ὡς ἐρώμενον, "It moves as being loved". This is obviously not love in the human sense, but more like magnetic attraction. (*Metaphysics*, p. 1072.) On the other hand ἄτοπον ἂν εἴη εἴ τις φαίη φιλεῖν τὸν Δία, "It would be absurd for anyone to say he felt an affection for Zeus". (*Magna Moralia*, 1208 b 30.)

love for his creature, mankind. They clung to this belief throughout the Middle Ages in spite of their equally firm belief in Hell. They cling to it still in spite of the obvious cruelty and imperfection of the world by which alone that ruler and creator makes himself known. They must insist on believing in the teeth of all the material evidence that "God is Love".

True, there is in all or almost all religions a violent difficulty when we insist that the God of love must also have perfect power. Nothing else will satisfy man's natural desire. The thing we cannot endure to think of is the omnipotence against us of the material or non-human world, with its utter disregard of what we call moral or spiritual values. God must deliver us from the body of that death, or else he fails us altogether. The simplest solution is a primitive dualism; if there is a friend, a good man, behind the phenomena, is there not equal plausibility, and better evidence, for supposing there is also an enemy, a bad man? God and Devil, Ormuzd and Ahriman, Jehovah and Satan the Adversary, always at strife, seem to afford a fair explanation of the world as we actually see it; our wish-thinking only insists that the end of the strife shall be an unconditional victory for the good. All the subtle explanations of modern theology really fail to provide us with a solution of the fundamental and glaring contradiction involved in all religions which maintain that a world, admitted to be full of evil, is created and ordered by the will of a being who is perfectly good and also omnipotent. The hypothesis of an "intractable material" which the good God cannot control is inconsistent with his omnipotence. The hypothesis that he left man's will free to do good or evil as it chose is inconsistent with his perfect goodness, and fails entirely to meet the difficulties presented by a "Nature red in tooth and claw with ravin", in which every creature normally lives by inflicting pain and death on others, and cannot live otherwise. Another hypothesis is that we are mistaken in supposing that there is any evil in the world: all is really just as it ought to be. Either no Jews are persecuted, no Chinese massacred, no men or animals perishing in torture, or, if there are, it is good for them, and if they had sense they would like it. This doctrine is, in its ordinary forms, heartless as well as senseless. It is not only obviously untrue, but like the doctrine of eternal damnation it is an untruth which, in the natural meaning of the words, no feeling man could believe. But there is another sense in which it can be understood and may, as far as logic goes, be true; only in that case it utterly wrecks the current conceptions of theism. It may be that what man calls "good" is not at all the same as what the Power behind the world calls "good". That Power may well be no more "good" or "just" or "merciful" than it is "polite" or "clever" or "agreeable" or a "good linguist". All our moral ideas may be as inapplicable to it as our social phrases and conventional prejudices. Such a Power is neither good nor evil, neither friend nor enemy. It cannot be loved or hated. It is not anthropomorphic, not human, not describable in human language—not what we mean by God.

Along another line of thought a particular form of man-thinking and wish-thinking has been progressively undermined and made, not exactly impossible, but at least destitute of its chief claim to probability. The greatest shock sustained by theistic religion in historical times was perhaps that which came with the astronomical discoveries of Copernicus. The thought of post-Aristotelian Greece, of Rome, of the Middle Ages, was permeated by the researches and doctrines of the great Hellenistic astronomers. "The stars, which had always moved men's wonder and even worship, were now seen and proved to be no wandering fires, but parts of an immense and apparently eternal Order or Cosmos. One star might differ from another star in glory, but they were all alike in their obedience to law. Their courses were laid down for them by a

Being greater than they. The Order or Cosmos was a proven fact; therefore the purpose implied in it was a proven fact; and, though in its completeness inscrutable, it could in part be divined from the observation that all these varied and eternal splendours had for their centre our Earth and its ephemeral master. The Purpose, though it is not our purpose, is especially concerned with us and circles round us. It is the purpose of a God who loves Man."[1]

On that conception the Stoic and Christian theologies were based. And now we know that it is not true. Our earth is not the centre of the cosmos; it is not even the centre of the solar system; and the solar system itself is only one out of very many systems, incalculably vast, incalculably numerous, to which the welfare or misery of us human beings is, as far as we can make out, of no consequence whatever. We are not the central care of the universe. The sun was not created to give us light by day, nor the moon by night. The animals were not, after all, made for man's sake, so as to provide him with food by eating them, with clothes by skinning them or with healthy amusement by trapping, hunting, shooting, and tormenting them. All such anthropocentric thinking proves to have been just a part of our inordinate human con-

[1] *Five Stages of Greek Religion*, p. 125.

ceit.[1] It is wish-thinking or fear-thinking. It is the same sort of thinking which, with no evidence whatever except wishes and fears, created an infinite reward for the good and the wicked, those who have pleased or displeased the gods of our imagination, those who are with us or against us.

What then? Must we say that all theism is a form of mere wish-thinking, the projection of man's own desires and fears, conditioned at every turn by the limitations of the human brain? The result is frightening. "If there are no gods", says Cicero, "or if such gods as there may be have no care for us, and pay no regard to our actions, what becomes of piety and religion?" And later: "I do not feel sure, if we cast away piety towards the gods, that Good Faith (*fides*) and all the associations of human life, and the best of virtues, Justice, may not perish with it" (*Nat. De.* i. 2). For one thing, Heaven and Hell

---

[1] Cf. Euripides, *Electra*, v. 726 ff. Old shepherds tell how the first sin committed on earth, Thyestes's theft of the Golden Lamb, convulsed all nature:

> "Then, then the world was changed,
> And the Father, where they ranged,
>   Shook the golden stars and glowing,
> And the great Sun stood deranged
>   In the glory of his going."

We and our contemporaries, he says, merely smile at such simplicity.

go. Is that a serious loss? It is hard to know how far considerations so remote and speculative have affected man's conduct. Legislators have generally found that men are not much influenced by promises of rewards or punishments to be realized even as far off as ten or twenty years hence. But, for what they may be worth, they go. More serious than that, the whole belief in a moral universe goes. We are left face to face with that "Nature red in tooth and claw" which cares neither for the type nor for the individual; with those aeonian processes which make not merely the life of the individual man but the whole existence of human beings on the earth little flashes of movement in the history of a small planet which itself must in due course pass away to nothingness. One may recall a classical Japanese Haikai describing the value of man in eternity:

> "In a still pool
> A frog jumped:
> A noise of splashing water!"

We see good men living strenuous lives for their fellows. We see St. Francis devoting all his powers to love and piety. We see man's conscience protesting against wrong, and resisting to the point of martyrdom. Is all that based on a mere delusion: is it mere wish-thinking to suppose that conscience really matters? In revulsion against such a thought comes a passionate rush of religious reaction, based usually not on reason but on emotional appeal. "See what a loathsome creature man is", says Pascal, "when once his divine guidance is taken away. See how divine he can be if he is safe in the fold of the Catholic Church." The appeal is unconvincing to most of us. Not only would it be difficult to prove that those who have firmly rejected the wiles of Protestants and Freemasons are more virtuous than those who have embraced them; but, as soon as the claim is made that orthodoxy is necessary to moral salvation, there are too many conflicting revelations in the field, each with its own authoritative orthodoxy. Granted that the true faith will save us, which of the fifty-odd Christian sects is the true faith, to say nothing of the religions of Judaism, Islam, Hinduism, Buddhism, or the various systems of China and Japan? Far more plausible, as well as more civilized, is the claim that all these warring sects may be trying, imperfectly and confusedly, to say the same thing: that there is a God of Love and Justice, that there is a personal being who, in spite of our crabbed logic, is in some sense higher than we can comprehend both All-good and All-powerful, if only we will lay down our mortal judgement and stake all on faith? Immensely attractive to almost everyone; and yet that is just the theism which we have been examining and have found to be anthropomorphic in its essence and based on a wish, not on evidence. Modern Indian philosophers, like Radhakrishnan, have expounded eloquently the theme that religion is not a set of doctrines; it is an experience. And religious experience is based on the realization of the "presence of the divine in man". "Dogma divides and sows enmity. Experience unites and makes concord. Dogma needs to be proven; experience needs no proof. It is a fact."

Alas! The experience may be a fact, but the interpretation of experience is something different. What we mean by "the divine in man" is, I fear, merely the same thing as the human in God; some sublimation of the highest human qualities which we have projected from ourselves on to the image of this intractably anthropomorphic god created by our own man-thinking and wish-thinking. It is our own dream returning to us in the guise of an external being.

Men accepting these somewhat mystical forms of belief are apt to find themselves professing or preaching some traditional theistic faith not quite because they believe it to be true, but because they are strongly convinced that it is good for other people to believe it; that in fact average human nature cannot get on without it.

The adherents of this line of thought inevitably find themselves confronted by a well-known problem: their creed, however it is expressed, means something quite different to the educated thinker and to the unthinking multitude. Cicero himself held the office of Augur: he considered it of the utmost importance that the Roman people should continue to observe the traditional pieties and sanctities of the Roman religion; he duly performed the rites and took the auspices. Yet, as we all remember, he quotes with approval Cato's expression of wonder that two *haruspices* can look each other in the face without laughing.[1] The priests of the modern Roman Church when presiding over certain miracles in the South of Italy may well feel the same difficulty as the *haruspices* did, and no doubt surmount it as successfully. So much most people will admit. But the position of that eminent and high-minded body of men, the Broad Church leaders of the nineteenth century, is open to a very similar criticism. Dr. Bridges in one of his essays[2] quotes certain passages from Dr. Jowett's thoughts on religion; for example: "*Limits of change within the Christian religion. The conception of miracles may become impossible and absurd. Immortality may pass into present consciousness of goodness and of God. The*

---

[1] *De Div.* ii. 51; cf. *Nat. De.* i. 71.
[2] Loc. cit., pp. 64 ff.

*personality of God may pass into an idea. Doctrines
may become unmeaning words."* And a little later:
*"Christianity has become one religion among many.
. . . We pray to God as a person; but there must
always be a* subintelligitur *that He is not a person.
Our forms of worship, public and private, imply
some interference with the course of Nature, (yet) we
know that the empire of law permeates all things."*
Dr. Jowett's High Church critics found it easy
to argue that such doctrines, or rather such
radical scepticisms, were inconsistent not merely
with the Articles of Faith which Dr. Jowett had
signed, but with the obvious implications of his
position as a clergyman of the Established Church.
His defence, that he was assisting in a vital
movement for the liberalizing and enlightening
of the Church, is a strong one, but not for the
moment relevant to our discussion. It is clear
that in these creeds with a *subintelligitur* attached,
we are not far from the position attributed by
Gibbon to the cultivated circles in Ancient
Rome, that all religions were to the uneducated
equally true, to the philosopher equally false,
and to the statesman equally useful. A position
which has a great deal to be said for it, but which
cannot satisfy a speculative mind determined to
preserve its honesty as well as its religious
emotion.

Is it possible for us to do both? One of the

Stoic arguments for the existence of the gods was the observation that, as a matter of fact, god-fearing or religious people live better and more successful lives than godless people, which would hardly be the case if they were wrong and the godless right in their main doctrine. A quaint piece of reasoning, but with some force in it. Man must at times be conscious of the vast mystery which surrounds his little island of knowledge; the inconceivable measures of astronomical distance, of the movement of light, of the extent of the wave-lengths which are neither visible to our eyes nor audible to our ears; the mere length of time involved in the history of man, of the earth, of the solar system. These things produce on any sensitive mind an impression of awe and a feeling not so much of the insignificance of all our human interests, but perhaps rather a doubt whether we can know what is significant or not. An individual's mental attitude towards this mystery is one of the most revealing things about him, revealing just because he has no certain information to go upon and therefore acts and feels according to the general bias of his character. Utterly to ignore the mystery is what the Stoics called "godless" or impious; yet, if we attempt to conceive it or speak of it, two results seem inescapable. In the first place, all our language will be metaphorical. To describe something utterly beyond our experience and power of conception we possess only words created by our experience to describe objects that we know. Secondly, though the material out of which we build our metaphorical Cosmos is no doubt our experience, the form we give it is determined, not by known facts, but entirely by our wishes or ideals. We build our conception of the divine out of what we take to be the best that we know or can imagine from our experience. What theists call "the goodness of God" and mystics "the divine in man" is precisely man's *humanitas*, the quality which specially exalts him above the beasts and progressively raises him higher and higher above himself.

This is essentially Comte's answer. He denies entirely that morality depends on any system of false beliefs, though of course it may often be accompanied by them. Morality is based on the results of many centuries and millennia of social experience and has its roots in human character. As for the belief in Hell and Heaven, it is not only not necessary as a basis for morality; it absolutely undermines morality. A good act done for the sake of a personal reward or under the terror of a personal chastisement loses much of its value as a good act. The whole supposition that a system of violent and intense rewards and punishments is necessary to induce human beings to perform acts for the good of others is based on a false psychology which starts from the individual isolated man instead of man the social animal. Man is an integral member of his group. Among his natural instincts there are those which aim at group-preservation as well as self-preservation; at the good of *autrui* as well as of *moi*. Even among the animals, a cow, a tigress, a hen pheasant, does not need a promise of future rewards to induce her to risk her life to save her young from harm. The male bison or gorilla needs no reward before fighting devotedly for his females and children. They all instinctively care for *autrui*. And it would be a mistake to imagine that this devotion only shows itself in the form of fighting, or only in dangerous crises. It is part of the daily life of any natural group or herd: the strong members help the weak, the weak run for protection to the strong. In man even in his primitive state these instincts are much more highly developed than in the gregarious animals; with the process of civilization they increase in range, in reasonableness, in sublimity. In the late war, how many thousands of men—not particularly selected or high-minded men—risked their lives eagerly to save a companion wounded in No Man's Land? They did not ask or know why they did it. Some may have alleged motives of religion, or motives of ambition in the form of medals or promotions. But the basic motive was probably more or less the same all through; that instinctively they could not see a mate lying there wounded and not try to help him. Why did St. Francis love his fellow-men, his birds, his enemies? He no doubt explained that it was all a part of his love of God. True, but his love of God was really his humanity, his *humanitas*, his ἀνθρωπότης, which made him love his group, and take into his group all life that met him, especially those parts that needed love most, the helpless, the despised, the angry and hostile. The humanity of man is an immense spirit, seen in the saints and heroes, seen in religious bodies; seen in dull prosaic societies of philanthropists trying, skilfully or blunderingly, to help the unfortunate; seen in the ordinary social life of families and peoples. *Deus est mortali iuvare mortalem*: "God is the helping of man by man"; or should we rather translate it: "The spirit of mutual help among all mortal beings is the true object of worship?"[1] That, says Comte, is what God is. Not an external all-powerful Person, who will show favour to those who obey Him and terrible wrath to those who offend Him; not even an imaginary Infinitely Good Man whom we must serve out of love for His goodness; but a perfectly real spirit of good-

[1] Pliny, *Nat. Hist.* ii. 7, 18.

ness, which runs in some degree through all life, but finds its highest expression in the best men, the spirit that we can only call *Humanitas*, Humanity.[1]

Where does the main difference lie between this faith and faith in a personal God? Only, I think, here: that in theism St. Francis or any martyr is held to be always on the winning side; sure of his victory, sure of his reward. I do not, of course, say that he practises virtue merely for the sake of his reward: but at least he is sure that he will have it. In Positivism he takes his risk. He performs his act of love or sacrifice for the sake of others and their good, whether in the end it be fruitful of good to himself or utterly wasted. He does not wait to risk his safety until he is assured of success.

Comte always insists on seeing man as a member of Society. In society is realized his three-fold slogan: *Love the principle*: without love, no society can exist. *Order the basis*: without order no

[1] An objection may be raised that, morally speaking, Man is in many ways not better but far worse than the beasts, certainly more licentious, treacherous, and cruel. If we worship "Humanity" must we not include these special human vices? The objection, so far as it is not merely verbal, is frivolous. What the Positivist proposes to worship is not everything that is characteristic of Man, but that quality, or that effort, by which Man is morally and intellectually higher than the beasts; exactly what Dr. Radhakrishnan means by "the divine in man".

society can continue. *Progress the end*: for every
human society by its own nature is imperfect
and aims at removing its imperfections, looking
higher as each flaw is cleared away. Comte is an
evolutionist not in the purely biological sense
but in the sociological; seeing the continuous
development of man's *Humanitas* to higher
achievement.

He calls this system a religion, not merely a
philosophy. Is this justified? For example, is
there a place in it for faith, for that "substance
of things hoped for, that evidence of things
unseen", which has been one of the most moving
forces of human history? History itself gives
abundant answers. Men have had faith in the
future of their country, faith in the cause for
which they worked, when those with less vision
could see no ground for faith. There is place for
faith, place for hope; most royal and abundant
place for charity. Is there a place for prayer?
Not if prayer is merely a petition for personal
favours, but ample place if prayer is, as it is in
most of the higher religions, a concentration of
thought and love upon our ideal of life. A place
for worship? The whole system is a religion of
worship, as can be seen, for example, in the
Calendar of great men, where we not merely
study and contemplate with reverence the actual
life and work of those who have been Servants of

Humanity, but above all, since each one of them has his faults, dedicate ourselves to the spirit which they imperfectly illustrate. He laid stress—most of us will say, too much stress—on the need of an organized liturgy and regular meetings of worship. He even kept the idea of sacraments, for entry to the Church, for marriage, and other occasions, using the word not in the ecclesiastical sense but in that of the Roman soldier's oath or *Sacramentum*: a solemn devotion of life to a great purpose.

It is not my business in this paper to try to point out particular weaknesses in Comte's vast system, or unattractive egotisms in his character. It may be that his literary style and the mind which it expressed were more conspicuous for rigid logic and strength than for sympathy and imagination. It may be that he was consciously or unconsciously inspired by Robespierre's curious project for leaving the Catholic Church fully established while removing the creeds. Certainly the system appeals more to those accustomed to the Catholic tradition than it does to Protestants. On the other hand he did try conscientiously to get free from the unconscious historic trammels in which the Christian tradition necessarily confines our Western civilization, and to speak intelligibly to Confucian, Muslim, or Buddhist. For my own part I cannot but think he attempted too much; he tried to build a great structure almost complete in detail when he had materials only for a foundation and some outside walls, and even those subject to reformation. But whatever the failures and imperfections of his actual statement, whatever the elements in it that will be superseded by future advances of thought, I cannot but feel, as did his contemporaries Mill, Morley, George Eliot, Spencer, as well as Bridges, Beesly, and Harrison, first, that his system forms a wonderful achievement of sincere and constructive thinking, and, secondly, that the thing he is trying to say, if only he could succeed in saying it, is not only sublime but true.